Tune In To God:

The Miracle Methods of Jesus

By

The Sending Love Club

This book is dedicated with Love to God who created us, to our parents and step-parents who raised us right, to our spouses who help to keep us on the path of Love, and to everyone else who gives us opportunities to Love.

Copyright © 2012 by Sending Love Club, LLC.

All rights reserved. No part of this publication may be reproduced, distributed, or transmitted in any form or by any means, including photocopying, recording, or other electronic or mechanical methods, without the prior written permission of the publisher, except in the case of brief quotations embodied in critical reviews and certain other noncommercial uses permitted by copyright law.

Table of Contents

Introduction 4

Method #1: Tune in to God by remembering God 9
Method #2: Tune in to God by sighing 19
Method #3: Tune in to God by feeling your heart 25
Method #4: Tune in to God by giving thanks 34
Method #5: Tune in to God by looking up 45
Method #6: Tune in to God by smiling 52
Method #7: Tune in to God by sending Love 57
Method #8: Tune in to God by forgiving 66
Method #9: Tune in to God by asking and believing 73
Method #10: Tune in to God by surrendering to God 81
Method #11: Tune in to God by remembering who you are ... 85
Method #12: Tune in to God with tunes 89
Method #13: Tune in to God with nature 94
Method #14: Tune in to God with silence 96
Method #15: Tune In To God with other people 102

Daily Practice 107

The Final Word 113

Transcript of Tuning In To God: An audio guide to the miracle methods of Jesus 115

Introduction

Our premise is that God is Infinite Eternal Almighty Divine Love.

Our theory is that the more one tunes in to God the better one's life is. We seem to have gotten out of tune with God. Like the prodigal son we have wandered away and forgotten our connection to God, forgotten who we really are. It is in our best interest to remember to tune in to God more often.

"Thou wilt keep him in perfect peace, whose mind is stayed on thee: because he trusteth in thee."
Isaiah 26:3
(All Bible quotations are from the King James Version unless otherwise indicated)

"The longer you grow in your relationship with the Lord, the easier it is to know when he's talking to you. The key is learning how to tune in to him."
Rick Warren, author of "A Purpose Driven Life"

Our methods are the methods that Jesus taught and used, as we understand them. Jesus was tuned in to God as no one else. He taught people to seek and to tune in to the Kingdom of God, the Kingdom of Heaven. When He and His followers used these methods miracles followed. These methods might just be worth trying! Even modern science is validating the positive effects of these methods. Some of these methods you have heard before, but some you may have overlooked.

The important thing is putting these methods into practice. They are simple to do and don't take much time. Spending a few minutes focusing on tuning in to God changes lives. Think of how much time you spend tuning in to television shows or worry thoughts in order to motivate yourself to take a few moments to tune in to God.

Like many musical instruments we tend to get out of tune. Stress, worry, distractions, and the concerns of this world can get us out of tune. The methods that Jesus taught and used are powerful tools for getting us in tune with God and His Kingdom.

Two apt analogies:

1. You are like a radio. Whatever station you are tuned in to is what you broadcast out. Tune to station WGOD (or KGOD if you are west of the Mississippi river) a little bit more of the time and you will experience a more blessed life.

"Be not deceived; God is not mocked: for whatsoever a man soweth, that shall he also reap."
Galatians 6:7

2. You are like a magnet. You usually tend to weakly attract whatever your attention focuses upon and are easily pulled by other influences. Tune in to and get aligned with the All-Powerful magnetic force (God/Divine Love) and then you are connected to the Almighty and all things are possible.

"I am the vine, ye are the branches: He that abideth in me, and I in him, the same bringeth forth much fruit: for without me ye can do nothing."
John 15:5

"And the glory which thou gavest me I have given them; that they may be one, even as we are one: I in them, and thou in me, that they may be made perfect in one; and that the world may know that thou hast sent me, and hast loved them, as thou hast loved me."

John 17:22-23

"But Jesus beheld them, and said unto them, With men this is impossible; but with God all things are possible."

Matthew 19:26

Our goal is to help everyone who wants to have a spiritual experience to have one; to help people to experience and be transformed by the Divine Love that is God. The way to experience Spirit and have a spiritual experience is to tune in to Spirit/God. Having a spiritual experience has been shown to help in recovery from addictions, to decrease depression and suicide, and to improve physical health and other circumstances — often in miraculous ways. Reading this book and listening to the soundtrack that guides you through these methods will help you to tune in to God - with a better life and world resulting. Pondering the Bible verses and quotations in this book has helped many to tune in to God.

The authors are a small group that gets together to tune in to God. We come from different backgrounds and faiths. Some of us are Methodists and are somewhat obsessed with methods. All of us believe that the methods that Jesus taught and used are powerful tools for transformation and healing and miracles.

"And Jesus said unto the centurion, Go thy way; and as thou hast believed, so be it done unto thee. And his servant was healed in the selfsame hour."

Matthew 8:13

"There are only two ways to live your life. One is as though nothing is a miracle. The other is as though everything is a miracle."

Albert Einstein

Some of us consider ourselves to be scientists. It is hoped that we can avoid theological arguments and debates. We want to focus on methods. We encourage you to try putting these methods into practice and see what happens. Try it, you'll like it!

So, how do we know if we are tuned in to God? We certainly don't have it all figured out, but it seems to have a lot to do with the heart:

"For as he thinketh in his heart, so is he:……."

Proverbs 23:7

"…for out of the abundance of the heart the mouth speaketh. A good man out of the good treasure of the heart bringeth forth good things…."
Matthew 12:34-35

And even more to do with Love:

"By this shall all men know that ye are my disciples, if ye have love one to another."

John 13:35

These methods that Jesus taught and used (if put into practice) will help to open, cleanse, and purify your heart and put you in tune with the Infinite Eternal Divine Love that is God. For many of us these methods help us to feel our heart "strangely warmed".

We are still learning how to better tune in to God and we would like to hear from you about what helps you to tune in to God. Writing to us implies permission to publish your method and initials on our website and in the planned "Tune In To God, volume 2: What works for you."

Write to us with your ideas, comments, questions, or prayer requests. We gather together to tune in to God and we ask for the Highest Good for those who write to us.

"Again, I say unto you, That if two of you shall agree on earth as touching anything that they shall ask, it shall be done for them of my Father which is in heaven. For where two or three are gathered together in my name, there am I in the midst of them."
Matthew 18:19-20

When you tune in to God with the miracle methods of Jesus you are plugged in to the ultimate, the only Power Source and your Love-Light shines, or God's Love and Light shine through you. Tune in to God and allow this Light to shine away any shadows of stress and limitation. And let the miracles become apparent!

This book was written as an afterthought. Our original project was to enable folks to have the *experience* of Divine Love/God in a way that you can't get from reading a book. We created what is now called <u>Tuning In To God: An audio guide to the miracle methods of Jesus</u> to guide people in using the methods that Jesus taught and used to tune in to and experience the Divine Love that is God. This book was written to elucidate the concepts and to provide scriptural and scientific support for the methods. You can order and/or download the audio from Amazon.com or our website.

Visit our website at **http://TuneIntoGod.com**

Email us at **Love{at}TuneIntoGod.com**

And Stay Tuned!!

Method #1

Tune in to God by remembering God

The first step to tune in to God is to remember God. We are all, as we say here in the South, "bad to forget."

We get distracted and tune in to worries, daydreams, memories, and pain and we forget God. It is human nature to pay attention to what is irritating you and it takes an effort to turn (repent) and to seek the Good, the Kingdom of Heaven which is at hand within you.

Do you want to tune in to God/Spirit/Divine Love or into worries and limitation?

"No man can serve two masters: for either he will hate the one, and love the other; or else he will hold to the one, and despise the other. Ye cannot serve God and mammon."
Matthew 6:24

If you are choosing to read this book then at least part of you is interested in tuning in to God.

Jesus reminded people of God and His Kingdom all the time — by His stories, His teachings, His actions, and by His very presence.

This project of remembering God has been seen as worthwhile by many wise people. Brother Lawrence, a 17th-century French monk called it "The Practice of the Presence of God."

"Believe me. Immediately make a holy and firm resolution never more to forget Him. Resolve to spend the rest of your days in His sacred presence, deprived of all consolations for the love of Him if He thinks fit. Set heartily about this work, and if you do it sincerely, be assured that you will soon find the effects of it."
Brother Lawrence

"Practicing the presence of God is a skill, a habit you can develop. Just as musicians practice scales every day in order to play beautiful music with ease, you must force yourself to think about God at different times in your day. You must train your mind to remember God."
Rick Warren

Emmet Fox called it "The Golden Key to Prayer" and said that it is the answer to all problems.

"As for the actual method of working, like all fundamental things, it is simplicity itself. All that you have to do is this: Stop thinking about the difficulty, whatever it is, and think about God instead. This is the complete rule, and if only you will do this, the trouble, whatever it is, will presently disappear."
Emmet Fox

But even if you remember to choose to tune in to God, what is your conception of God? Is God a bearded old man sitting in heaven judging and punishing people? Or a loving Father?

Just remembering and pondering God and His attributes helps you to tune in to God.

Here are some attributes of the God that Jesus was tuned in to and reminded others to tune in to:

God is Love

Jesus and the apostles reminded people of the loving nature of God.

"I in them, and thou in me, that they may be made perfect in one; and that the world may know that thou hast sent me, and hast loved them, as thou hast loved me."

John 17:23

"He that loveth not knoweth not God; for God is love."

1 John 4:8

"And we have known and believed the love that God hath to us. God is love; and he that dwelleth in love dwelleth in God, and God in him."

1 John 4:16

"Finally, brethren, farewell. Be perfect, be of good comfort, be of one mind, live in peace; and the God of love and peace shall be with you."

2 Corinthians 13:11

"…because the love of God is shed abroad in our hearts by the Holy Ghost which is given unto us."

Romans 5:5

"For God so loved the world, that he gave his only begotten Son, that whosoever believeth in him should not perish, but have everlasting life."

John 3:16

God is the Loving Father

Jesus called God by the Aramaic term "Abba" which is an endearing term for father, similar to our word "Daddy" or "Papa."

Jesus' parable of the prodigal son is one of the best depictions of our human predicament. We have wandered away from God. We have forgotten God and gotten distracted and we suffer. But all we need to do is turn (repent) toward our Loving Father and we are blessed beyond our best dreams.

"And he arose, and came to his father. But when he was yet a great way off, his father saw him, and had compassion, and ran, and fell on his neck, and kissed him."

Luke 15:20

"Doubtless thou art our father, though Abraham be ignorant of us, and Israel acknowledge us not: thou, O LORD, art our father, our redeemer; thy name is from everlasting."

Isaiah 63:16

God is Omniscient

"...God is greater than our heart, and knoweth all things."

1 John 3:20

"Great is our lord, and of great power: his understanding is infinite."

Psalm 147:5

"The eyes of the LORD are in every place, beholding the evil and the good."

Proverbs 15:3

God is All-Powerful

"But Jesus beheld them, and said unto them, with men this is impossible; but with God all things are possible."

Matthew 19:26

"I know that thou canst do every thing, and that no thought can be withholden from thee."

Job 42:2

"And I heard as it were the voice of a great multitude, and as the voice of many waters, and as the voice of mighty thunderings, saying, Alleluia: for the Lord God omnipotent reigneth."

Revelation 19:6

God is Omnipresent

"Whither shall I go from thy spirit? or whither shall I flee from thy presence? If I ascend up into heaven, thou art there: if I make my bed in hell, behold, thou art there. If I take the wings of the morning, and dwell in the uttermost parts of the sea; Even there shall thy hand lead me, and thy right hand shall hold me."

Psalm 139:7-10

"Am I a God at hand, saith the LORD, and not a God afar off? Can any hide himself in secret places that I shall not see him? saith the LORD. Do not I fill heaven and earth? saith the LORD."

Jeremiah 23:23-24

"For in him we live, and move, and have our being;"

Acts 17:28

God is available

"Now after that John was put in prison, Jesus came into Galilee, preaching the gospel of the kingdom of God, And saying, The time is fulfilled, and the kingdom of God is at hand: repent ye, and believe the gospel."

Mark 1:14-15

"...for he hath said, I will never leave thee, nor forsake thee."

Hebrews 13:5

"...for the LORD thy God, he it is that doth go with thee; he will not fail thee, nor forsake thee."

Deuteronomy 31:6

"Yea, though I walk through the valley of the shadow of death, I will fear no evil: for Thou art with me; Thy rod and Thy staff they comfort me."

Psalm 23:4

God is a God of miracles

"Jesus answered and said unto them, Go and shew John again those things which ye do hear and see: The blind receive their sight, and the lame walk, the lepers are cleansed, and the deaf hear, the dead are raised up, and the poor have the gospel preached to them."

Matthew 11:4-5

"Thou art the God that doest wonders: thou hast declared thy strength among the people."

Psalm 77:14

"And God wrought special miracles by the hands of Paul."

Acts 19:11

"And Stephen, full of faith and power, did great wonders and miracles among the people."

Acts 6:8

God is eternal and everlasting

"In the beginning was the Word, and the Word was with God, and the Word was God. The same was in the beginning with God."

John 1:1-2

"O give thanks unto the LORD, for he is good: for his mercy endureth for ever."

Psalm 107:1

"But thou, O LORD, shalt endure for ever; and thy remembrance unto all generations."

Psalm 102:12

"Lord, thou hast been our dwelling place in all generations. Before the mountains were brought forth, or ever thou hadst formed the earth and the world, even from everlasting to everlasting, thou art God."

Psalm 90:1-2

"I am Alpha and Omega, the beginning and the ending, saith the Lord, which is, and which was, and which is to come, the Almighty."

Revelation 1:8

God is Good

God is so Good.
God is so Good.
God is so Good.
He's so Good to me.
Traditional folk hymn

God is so Good.
God is so Good.
God is so Good.
He's so Good through me.
The authors

"And Jesus said unto him, Why callest thou me good? There is none good but one, that is, God."

Mark 10:18

"As newborn babes, desire the sincere milk of the word, that ye may grow thereby: If so be ye have tasted that the Lord is gracious."

1 Peter 2:2-3

God is Spirit

"God is a Spirit: and they that worship him must worship him in spirit and in truth."

John 4:24

"Know ye not that ye are the temple of God, and that the Spirit of God dwelleth in you?"

1 Corinthians 3:16

"For as many as are led by the Spirit of God, they are the sons of God."

Romans 8:14

"But if I cast out devils by the Spirit of God, then the kingdom of God is come unto you."

Matthew 12:28

God is merciful and forgiving and kind and giving

"If ye then, being evil, know how to give good gifts unto your children: how much more shall your heavenly Father give the Holy Spirit to them that ask him?"

Luke 11:13

"...for your heavenly Father knoweth that ye have need of all these things. But seek ye first the kingdom of God, and his righteousness; and all these things shall be added unto you."

Matthew 6:32-33

"For great is thy mercy toward me: and thou hast delivered my soul from the lowest hell."

Psalm 86:13

"For thou, Lord, art good, and ready to forgive; and plenteous in mercy unto all them that call upon thee."

Psalm 86:5

God is Light

"This then is the message which we have heard of him, and declare unto you, that God is light, and in him is no darkness at all."

1 John 1:5

"In him was life; and the life was the light of men. And the light shineth in darkness; and the darkness comprehended it not."

John 1:4-5

"But ye are a chosen generation, a royal priesthood, an holy nation, a peculiar people; that ye should shew forth the praises of him who hath called you out of darkness into his marvelous light..."

1 Peter 2:9

"Every good gift and every perfect gift is from above, and cometh down from the Father of lights, with whom is no variableness, neither shadow of turning."

James 1:17

Just remembering these attributes and qualities of God helps you to tune in to God and can open the door to allow miracles in your life.

"Work by rehearsing anything or everything that you know about God. God is Wisdom, Truth, inconceivable Love. God is present everywhere; has infinite power; knows everything; and so on. It matters not how well you may think you understand these things; go over them repeatedly."

Emmet Fox, "The Golden Key to Prayer"

Validation of this method from modern science

Herbert Benson, M.D., Dean Ornish, M.D., Larry Dossey, M.D., and many others have done research that shows that people who have spiritual beliefs and practices live longer and recover faster from illness and adversity than those who don't.

Memory research has shown that repetition is one of the strongest factors in determining what is remembered. What is repeated more often is more likely to be remembered. Another strong finding in memory research is that distributed practice is more powerful than massed practice. So it is better to spend a little time every day tuning in to God than for a longer period once per week. In other words, read some of books like this one and tune in to God with these miracle methods of Jesus daily.

Putting the method into practice

Remember God. Ponder God's attributes and qualities. Read about matters spiritual. Read inspired and inspiring materials (like this book).

Listen to uplifting music and watch uplifting video. Pray, chant, sing, whatever reminds you and turns your attention toward God.

Set aside a particular time to remember and tune in to God.

Practice, practice, practice these miracle methods of Jesus.

Remember that you are loved more than you can possibly comprehend. Feel that feeling of being loved. Now you are tuning in to God.

Method #2

Tune in to God by sighing

Breath is life.

"And the LORD God formed man of the dust of the ground, and breathed into his nostrils the breath of life; and man became a living soul."
Genesis 2:7

"The Spirit of God hath made me, and the breath of the Almighty hath given me life."
Job 33:4

Breath is Spirit. The word for breath is the same as the word for Spirit in most languages. This is the case for the Hebrew and Greek languages in which the Bible was written and the Aramaic language that Jesus spoke.

"God is a Spirit: and they that worship him must worship him in spirit and in truth."
John 4:24

Many, many saints, mystics, monks, nuns and others have used breathing exercises, breath prayers, and other techniques involving the breath in efforts to tune in to and realize the Divine. There are volumes and volumes written on practices such as rhythmic breathing, connected breathing, breath awareness, rapid breathing, and even alternate-nostril breathing.

Jesus is the Master of simplicity. The only breathing technique that is described as being used by Him in the Bible is the sigh…….and a miracle followed.

"And looking up to heaven, he sighed, and saith unto him, Ephphatha, that is, Be opened. And straightway his ears were opened, and the string of his tongue was loosed, and he spake plain."

Mark 7:34-35

Let us examine the sigh.

To sigh is to inhale a larger quantity of air than usual and immediately expel it, breathing out more completely and usually audibly. Infants sigh on a fairly regular basis and it has been shown that sighing helps to develop and strengthen the lungs.

Adults in modern societies tend to breathe very poorly. We usually exhale less than half of the air in our lungs and therefore breathe in relatively little fresh air to the detriment of our physical, emotional, mental, and spiritual health. Restrictive clothing, obesity, poor posture, and poor breathing habits all contribute to less-than-optimal breathing. We have forgotten how to breathe!

"One way to break up any kind of tension is good deep breathing."

Byron Nelson

Exhaling is so important. In breathing, as in many other arenas, it is more blessed to give than to receive. In clinical studies with thousands of people observed over several decades it has been shown that forced exhalation volume is the best predictor of mortality and longevity. And a sigh is a great way to exhale more fully and hence breathe more deeply.

"Learn how to exhale, the inhale will take care of itself."

Carla Melucci Ardito

Sub-optimal breathing also affects our mind and emotions. When we are stressed or fearful we stop breathing or breathe shallowly. And shallow breathing contributes to less alertness and more stress.

"In my experience, stress is a primary cause, or an aggravating cause, of most cases of illness. And even if people have diseases that clearly have organic physical causes, relaxation can nonetheless benefit them and help their body's healing system work better. And I think that all people in our culture can benefit from learning to relax... Of all the techniques that I have investigated for reducing stress and increasing relaxation, it is breath work that I have found to be the most time-efficient, the most cost-efficient and the one that most promotes increased wellness and optimal health. In addition, working with the breath can be a very powerful technique to center the mind, to help you work more effectively, to help you deal with all of the challenges that life throws in your way every day..."
From Andrew Weil's recording, "Breathing, The Master Key to Self Healing"

The simple sigh that Jesus used can be a key to improved physical, mental, and emotional health as well as spiritual growth. Sighing can help you tune in to God.

For this method, we will breathe through the nose, if possible. Begin by just becoming more aware of your breathing. Can you hear your breathing? Can you feel the air as it passes in and out through your nostrils?

Next, we will sigh. Inhale, letting the ribs move outward (not pulling in the stomach) and then filling the lungs more completely, feeling the chest expand and collarbones lift. Then without pausing exhale with an audible sigh and breathe out slowly and more completely than usual, now pulling in the stomach to push out even more air. Just two or three of these sighs will oxygenate your body and brain and open and cleanse your heart.

> "As the hart panteth after the water brooks, so panteth my soul after thee, O God."
>
> *Psalm 42:1*

Feel your heart lifting as you inhale... and feel any burdens on your heart being dropped as you exhale.

> "Create in me a pure heart, O God, and renew a steadfast spirit within me."
>
> *Psalm 51:10*

After a few sighs, return to breathing normally. As you get in the habit of sighing a few times per day, you will be training yourself to breathe more deeply.

> "There is one way of breathing that is shameful and constricted. Then, there's another breath of love that takes you all the way to infinity."
>
> *Rumi*

There are different types of sighs. There are sighs of frustration, sighs of boredom, sighs of grief, and sighs of exhaustion. Our sigh, the sigh of Jesus, is a sigh of relief and joy. Especially after remembering the attributes of God and His Love for us, when we sigh we are sighing a sigh of relief and joy that God is on the scene, that Divine Love is in charge, and that the Kingdom of Heaven is at hand.

While the wife of one of the authors has repeatedly assured him that *size* doesn't matter, we all agree that *sighs* matter.

Practice sighing. Sigh and let go. Let go and let God. Remember to exhale more completely.

> "The key is giving, tithing. Instead of trying to get all the oxygen you can — most of us do this and don't breathe out completely enough — focus on being a carbon dioxide giver/producer — helping plants."
>
> *Dr. Dean Ornish, M.D.*

Try adding an intention to your sigh. Say to yourself, "I am" as you inhale and "Love" as you sigh and exhale slowly and more completely. This is the "I Am Love Breath".

Some people have called this method a breath prayer and it is a powerful way to tune in to God.

"God wants us to connect with Him on a moment-by-moment basis. When we pray once a week or even once a day, we fail to take advantage of everything God has for us! Breath prayers are a great way to keep in contact with our Heavenly Father throughout our day. Just repeat short heart-felt prayers, such as "You are my God," "I love you Lord," and "Thank You, Jesus.""

Rick Warren, author of "A Purpose-Driven Life"

Other possibilities for intentional sighs or breath prayers:
"God Is" on the in-breath….."I am" on the out-breath.
"God is Love" on the in-breath….."I am loving" on the out-breath.
"I am" on the in-breath….."Loved" on the out-breath.
"God is Love" on the in-breath….."God is Light" on the out-breath.
"I am Love" on the in-breath….. "I am Light" on the out- breath.
"God is All There Is" on the in-breath…… "I am one with God" on the out-breath.

Try those on for sighs… and/or make up your own.

Another instance in the Gospels where Jesus' breathing is mentioned involves the Holy Spirit.

"Then said Jesus to them again, Peace be unto you: as my Father hath sent me, even so send I you. And when he had said this, he breathed on them, and saith unto them, Receive ye the Holy Ghost…"

John 20:21-22

Breathing was important to Jesus and the sigh is a method that can help you tune in to God and open and cleanse your heart, as we will see in the next chapter.

Breathing more deeply will improve your physical, emotional, and mental health.

Sighing like Jesus did, especially when combined with His other miracle methods can change your life in miraculous ways.

Sigh two or three more times. Breathe in fully and deeply – letting your abdomen and then your chest area expand, then relax and exhale with an audible sigh and exhale more completely. Listen to the sigh. Hear this sigh of relief and joy – that God is on the scene and in charge. Now breathe normally... and continue to listen... Notice if you can still hear your breathing... Take a moment to just breathe... and listen...

Validation from modern science

The Framingham Heart Study is one of the most famous and scientifically rigorous studies of a large population over an extended time. In this study it was found that breathing and lung capacity (forced exhalation volume) were the best predictors of how long a person will live.

Deeper breathing, diaphramatic breathing and other breathing techniques have been shown to improve hypertension, anxiety, pain, obesity, depression and dozens of other conditions that are caused or worsened by stress.

At least nine out of ten doctors, when asked, recommend daily breathing.

Putting the method into practice

Practice sighing a few times, several times per day. Remember to exhale more completely, pulling in your stomach a little (work those abs!)

Ponder the Infinity of Divinity, the Loving Father God and breathe a sigh of relief that All-powerful God is in charge and you are in Good hands.

Play around with some breath prayers.

One of our favorites is the I Am Love Breath:

Breathe in, lifting your heart and saying to yourself "I am" and then sigh and breathe out intending "Love" and keep breathing out Love 'til you can't breathe out no more. Repeat.

There are other breathing techniques that can be used to help one feel, energize, and purify the heart, but for now we will stick with the one that Jesus used. Especially when combined with some of His other methods, it helps us tune in to God.

Remember that you are loved more than you ever imagined and breathe a sigh of relief and joy.

Method #3

Tune in to God by feeling your heart

God and Jesus are all about Love.

The heart is associated with love in most cultures.

Jesus reminded people about the importance of the heart.

"Blessed are the pure in heart: for they shall see God."
Matthew 5:8

Most of us are not consciously tuned in to God/Divine Love most of the time. Not coincidentally, most of us are unaware of our heart most of the time. We have forgotten our heart and would benefit from being more aware of it.

The sigh that we practiced in the last chapter is a wonderful way to become more aware of, to open, and to purify the heart.

"Create in me a clean heart, O God; and renew a right spirit within me."
Psalm 51:10

"Draw nigh to God, and he will draw nigh to you. Cleanse your hands, ye sinners; and purify your hearts, ye double minded."
James 4:8

You may have noticed this already. As you continue to practice breathing more deeply and sighing you will be able to feel your heart beating in your chest—especially as you extend the exhalation and breathe out slowly and more completely. There is no need to hold your breath. Just sigh and breathe out slowly and more completely and place your attention in your heart region.

"Stand in awe, and sin not: commune with your own heart upon your bed, and be still. Selah."

Psalm 4:4

"I call to remembrance my song in the night: I commune with mine own heart: and my spirit made diligent search."

Psalm 77:6

Just being aware of your heartbeat is calming and therapeutic. It can also help you to tune in to God.

Now we are going to deepen our breathing a little bit more.

After a more complete exhale, make sure you fill your lungs from the bottom, letting your stomach and ribcage expand. Then breathe in a little bit more, feeling your heart region and collarbones lifting slightly. Then sigh and exhale slowly and deeply, feeling your heartbeat.

This is literally a heartfelt sigh.

"Remember: Nothing begets wholeness in life better than a heartfelt sigh."

Rebbe Nachman of Breslov

Feel your heart lifting up as you inhale...

And as you sigh and exhale you can feel your heart being unburdened and lightened. Feel the weight of your worries being dropped.

Don't be downhearted. Sigh a heartfelt sigh of relief that God is in charge and let your heart be lifted.

"Be on guard, so that your hearts will not be weighted down with dissipation and drunkenness and the worries of life, and that day will not come on you suddenly like a trap;"
Luke 21:34 (New American Standard Bible)

"Let us lift up our heart with our hands unto God in the heavens."
Lamentations 3:41

"A little lifting of the heart suffices; a little remembrance of God, one act of inward worship are prayers which, however short, are nevertheless acceptable to God."
Brother Lawrence from "The Practice of the Presence of God"

"Lift up your heart, lift up your voice; Rejoice; again I say, Rejoice!"
From the hymn "Rejoice, The Lord is King" by Charles Wesley

"My defence is of God, which saveth the upright in heart."
Psalm 7:10

"Light is sown for the righteous, and gladness for the upright in heart."
Psalm 97:11

With each breath, each sigh, you feel your heart being purified and cleansed.

"Blessed are the pure in heart: for they shall see God."
Matthew 5:8

"Truly God is good to Israel, even to such as are of a clean heart."
Psalm 73:1

"Now the end of the commandment is charity out of a pure heart, and of a good conscience, and of faith unfeigned…"
1 Timothy 1:5

Don't overdo it on sighing. Give a few heartfelt sighs and then breathe normally for a while. You are gradually training yourself to breathe more deeply.

Try placing one of your hands over your heart and send Love and appreciation and thanks to your heart. Your heart pumps out life-giving blood and Love and energy 24 hours per day, 365 days per year (366 days per year during leap years) and we just don't appreciate our hearts enough.

"For it is a good thing that the heart be established with grace;"
Hebrews 13:9

"He that loveth pureness of heart, for the grace of his lips the king shall be his friend."
Proverbs 22:11

Most of us have built walls around our hearts. When we have been hurt or scared we reacted by tensing and we tried to protect our heart by putting up a wall. But this wall prevents the Love of God from flowing to us and through us. It hardens our hearts so that we become to some degree unfeeling, unforgiving, resentful.

"Because that, when they knew God, they glorified him not as God, neither were thankful; but became vain in their imaginations, and their foolish heart was darkened."
Romans 1:21

Jesus reminded people to not have a hardened heart.

"Therefore they could not believe, because that Esaias said again, He hath blinded their eyes, and hardened their heart; that they should not see with their eyes, nor understand with their heart, and be converted, and I should heal them."
John 12:39-40

As you breathe deeply and sigh, imagine a beautiful light shining out of your heart in all directions. Feel Love flowing through your heart all around. With each breath, imagine the light getting brighter and expanding.

"For God, who commanded the light to shine out of darkness, hath shined in our hearts, to give the light of the knowledge of the glory of God in the face of Jesus Christ."
2 Corinthians 4:6

"Light is sown for the righteous, and gladness for the upright in heart."
Psalm 97:11

"Beauty is not in the face; beauty is light in the heart."
Kahlil Gibran

"A light heart lives long."
William Shakespeare

Let this Light and Love melt and dissolve the walls you have built around your heart. You can now breathe more freely. As you breathe in more deeply you feel your heart lifting and as you sigh and exhale more completely you feel all of the burdens and pain that you have been carrying in your heart being dropped, dissolved, shined away.

"Come unto me, all ye that labour and are heavy laden, and I will give you rest. For my yoke is easy, and my burden is light."
Matthew 11:28, 30

As you continue breathing more deeply and sighing you may feel what many people describe as an energy in the heart region. Some people report that they feel that their heart region is magnetized. Some describe it as a tingle or warmth.

"I felt my heart strangely warmed."
John Wesley

"And they said one to another, Did not our heart burn within us, while he talked with us by the way, and while he opened to us the scriptures?"
Luke 24:32

"A joyful heart is the inevitable result of a heart burning with love."
Mother Teresa

"A new heart also will I give you, and a new spirit will I put within you: and I will take away the stony heart out of your flesh, and I will give you an heart of flesh."
Ezekiel 36:26

Sighing like Jesus did stokes the fire in your heart so that the Love-Light of the Infinite Creator shines brighter.

Being aware of your heart and allowing your heart to be cleansed and purified by the heartfelt sigh tunes you in to God.

Feeling your heart, feeling the feeling of your heart being "strangely warmed" or magnetized is a key to powerful prayer and being tuned in to God.

Then shall ye call upon me, and ye shall go and pray unto me, and I will hearken unto you. And ye shall seek me, and find me, when ye shall search for me with all your heart.
Jeremiah 29:12-13

For some of us bowing our head helps us to be more aware of our heart. Do some experimentation. See what works for you.

"If love is in our hearts, every thought, word, and deed can bring about a miracle. Because understanding is the very foundation of love, words and actions that emerge from our love are always helpful.
Thich Nhat Hanh

Validation from modern science

Numerous studies have shown the benefits to babies of listening to recordings of heartbeats and feeling the heartbeat of a caregiver. Adults also benefit from listening to and/or feeling a heartbeat. And you have this valuable therapeutic tool within you.

The Heartmath Institute has conducted extensive research over the past 20 years showing that awareness of one's heartbeat and breath can have beneficial effects on physical and mental health.

Putting the method into practice

Ponder the Infinite Eternal Divine Love that is God. Remember that you are loved more than you can comprehend.

Breathe a deep sigh of relief that God is in charge and feel your heart beating as you exhale slowly and more completely.

Breathe in deeply from your abdomen and then breathe in a little more letting your heart region and collarbones lift slightly.

Sigh and exhale slowly allowing all of your worries to be released.

As you allow the exhale to slow and extend, feel your heart beating in your chest.

Just be aware of your heart region and notice if you feel a warmth or an energy or a tingling.

Do the I Am Love Breath:

Breathe in "I am" as you fill your lungs and lift your heart. Sigh and breathe out, intending "Love, Love, Love, Love..." with one "Love" for each heartbeat until you can't breathe out any more.

Feeling this heartfelt Love tunes you in to God and aligns you with the Divine.

Say aloud the words, "I invite God into my heart. I invite Divine Love into my heart. I allow God's Love to flow through me."

Bless your heart!

Remember you are loved sooooooooooooooooo much!!!!

Method #4

Tune in to God by giving thanks

"It is a good thing to give thanks unto the LORD..."
Psalm 92:1

Jesus was big on giving thanks.

And with Jesus, the giving of thanks often happened just prior to the occurrence of miracles. Giving thanks is a wonderful way to tune in to God.

"Then they took away the stone from the place where the dead was laid. And Jesus lifted up his eyes, and said, Father, I thank thee that thou hast heard me. And I knew that thou hearest me always: but because of the people which stand by I said it, that they may believe that thou hast sent me. And when he thus had spoken, he cried with a loud voice, Lazarus, come forth. And he that was dead came forth..."
John 11:41-44

"He told the crowd to sit down on the ground. When he had taken the seven loaves and given thanks, he broke them and gave them to his disciples to set before the people, and they did so. They had a few small fish as well; he gave thanks for them also and told the disciples to distribute them. The people ate and were satisfied. Afterward the disciples picked up seven basketfuls of broken pieces that were left over. About four thousand men were present..."
Mark 8:6-9

"Taking the five loaves and the two fish and looking up to heaven, he gave thanks and broke them. Then he gave them to the disciples to set before the people. They all ate and were satisfied, and the disciples picked up twelve basketfuls of broken pieces that were left over."

Luke 9:16-17 (New International Version)

Giving thanks helps one to tune in to the Infinite Eternal Creator God. It is Good to tune in to God. Good happens when one is tuned in to the Source of All Good.

Jesus taught the disciples:

"Therefore I say unto you, What things soever ye desire, when ye pray, believe that ye receive them, and ye shall have them."

Mark 11:24

And while this teaching does not explicitly mention being thankful, it is implied. How would you *feel* if you had received what you asked for? You would feel thankful! And this *feeling* of being thankful is a key to the realization.

"Asking is the seed; the feeling of thanks is the water. God is the sunshine (Love and Light)."

The authors

Remember to be thankful. Being thankful tunes you in to God and puts you in the flow of His blessings and Love.

It is very, very important to remember to Whom you are giving thanks.

"At that time Jesus answered and said, I thank thee, O Father, Lord of heaven and earth, because thou hast hid these things from the wise and prudent, and hast revealed them unto babes."

Matthew 11:25

If you remember that God, the Lord of heaven and earth, is Infinite, Eternal, and All-Powerful it is natural to feel awed and amazed. And when you remember that you are loved and cared for by this Infinity of Divinity and His angels it is difficult to imagine not feeling thankful and joyful.

Being thankful is so important. And none of us does it as much as is warranted. We take so much for granted. We are loved by the Infinite Creator more than we can comprehend, so we can obviously not be as thankful as we should be. But that's okay. Just making an effort to tune in to God by being a little more thankful will have amazingly wonderful effects upon your life.

The scriptures that Jesus learned from childhood and which he often quoted in His teachings emphasize again and again the importance of praise and thanksgiving.

"O give thanks unto the LORD; for he is good; for his mercy endureth for ever."

1 Chronicles 16:34

"I will praise the LORD according to his righteousness: and will sing praise to the name of the LORD most high."

Psalm 7:17

"Offer unto God thanksgiving; and pay thy vows unto the most High:"

Psalm 50:14

"I thank thee, and praise thee, O thou God of my fathers, who hast given me wisdom and might, and hast made known unto me now what we desired of thee: for thou hast now made known unto us the king's matter."

Daniel 2:23

"Rejoice in the LORD, ye righteous; and give thanks at the remembrance of his holiness."

Psalm 97:12

"I will praise the name of God with a song, and will magnify him with thanksgiving."
Psalm 69:30

"Unto thee, O God, do we give thanks, unto thee do we give thanks: for that thy name is near thy wondrous works declare."
Psalm 75:1

"O give thanks unto the LORD; for he is good: for his mercy endureth for ever.
O give thanks unto the God of gods: for his mercy endureth for ever.
O give thanks to the Lord of lords: for his mercy endureth for ever."
Psalm 136:1-3

"Praise the Lord! Thank the Lord because he is good. His love continues forever."
Psalm 106:1

"Enter into his gates with thanksgiving, and into his courts with praise: be thankful unto him, and bless his Name."
Psalm 100:4

And the shortest chapter of the Bible:

"O praise the LORD, all ye nations: praise him, all ye people. For his merciful kindness is great toward us: and the truth of the LORD endureth for ever. Praise ye the LORD."
Psalm 117

And we are also reminded of this powerful practice of giving thanks in the New Testament.

"Continue in prayer, and watch in the same with thanksgiving;"
Colossians 4:2

"And let the peace of God rule in your hearts, to the which also ye are called in one body; and be ye thankful."
Colossians 3:15

"Saying, We give thee thanks, O Lord God Almighty, which art, and wast, and art to come; because thou hast taken to thee thy great power, and hast reigned."

Revelation 11:17

"And were continually in the temple, praising and blessing God. Amen."

Luke 24:53

"But God be thanked, that ye were the servants of sin, but ye have obeyed from the heart that form of doctrine which was delivered you."

Romans 6:17

"Rejoice evermore. Pray without ceasing. In every thing give thanks: for this is the will of God in Christ Jesus concerning you."

1 Thessalonians 5:16-18

"Rejoice in the Lord alway: and again I say, Rejoice. Let your moderation be known unto all men. The Lord is at hand. Be careful for nothing; but in every thing by prayer and supplication with thanksgiving let your requests be made known unto God. And the peace of God, which passeth all understanding, shall keep your hearts and minds through Christ Jesus."

Philippians 4:4-7

Many other wise people have also recognized and emphasized the importance and power of giving thanks. Pondering some of these words of wisdom will help you to tune in to God.

"God gave you a gift of 86,400 seconds today. Have you used one to say "thank you?""

William A. Ward

"Wake at dawn with a winged heart and give thanks for another day of loving."

Kahlil Gibran

"Saying thank you is more than good manners. It is good spirituality."

Alfred Painter

"Some people have a wonderful capacity to appreciate again and again, freshly and naively, the basic goods of life, with awe, pleasure, wonder, and even ecstasy."

Abraham Maslow

"In daily life, we must see that it is not happiness that makes us grateful, but gratefulness that makes us happy."

Brother David Steindl-Rast

"I find that the more willing I am to be grateful for the small things in life, the bigger stuff just seems to show up from unexpected sources, and I am constantly looking forward to each day with all the surprises that keep coming my way!"

Louise L. Hay

"A grateful mind is a great mind which eventually attracts to itself great things."

Plato

"When a person doesn't have gratitude, something is missing in his or her humanity. A person can almost be defined by his or her attitude toward gratitude."

Elie Wiesel

"The essence of all beautiful art, all great art, is gratitude."

Friedrich Nietzsche

"The hardest arithmetic to master is that which enables us to count our blessings."

Eric Hoffer

"If you concentrate on finding whatever is good in every situation, you will discover that your life will suddenly be filled with gratitude, a feeling that nurtures the soul."

Rabbi Harold Kushner

"He is a wise man who does not grieve for the things which he has not, but rejoices for those which he has."

Epictetus

"When you arise in the morning, think of what a precious privilege it is to be alive — to breathe, to think, to enjoy, to love."
Marcus Aurelius

"A sensible thanksgiving for mercies received is a mighty prayer in the Spirit of God. It prevails with Him unspeakably."
John Bunyan

"Good men and bad men differ radically. Bad men never appreciate kindness shown them, but wise men appreciate and are grateful. Wise men try to express their appreciation and gratitude by some return of kindness, not only to their benefactor, but to everyone else."
Buddha

"Give thanks for unknown blessings already on their way."
Native American saying

"When I started counting my blessings, my whole life turned around."
Willie Nelson

"The first who will be summoned to paradise are those who have praised God in every circumstance."
Traditional Islamic saying

"The greatest saint in the world is not he who prays most or fasts most; it is not he who gives alms, or is most eminent for temperance, chastity or justice. It is he who is most thankful to God."
William Law

"Reflect upon your present blessings, of which every man has plenty; not on your past misfortunes of which all men have some."
Charles Dickens

"Gratitude is an opener of locked-up blessings."
Marianne Williamson

"Gratitude is not only the greatest of virtues, but the parent of all the others."

Cicero, Ancient Roman Lawyer

"Gratitude is the sign of noble souls."

Aesop

"Cultivate the habit of being grateful for every good thing that comes to you, and to give thanks continuously. And because all things have contributed to your advancement, you should include all things in your gratitude."

Ralph Waldo Emerson

"Acknowledging the good that you already have in your life is the foundation for all abundance."

Eckhart Tolle

Even in the most dire-seeming circumstances there is much for which to be thankful. We just need some reminders sometimes.

Validation from modern science

The relatively new field of study called Positive Psychology has conducted quite a bit of research on the concept of gratitude.

Studies have shown evidence that gratitude can improve physical, emotional, and mental health. People who report feeling more thankful appear to be happier, sleep better, have stronger immune systems, make more money, and have more energy than those who feel less thankful.

Dr. Robert Emmons from the University of California, Davis, in his book, "Thanks! How The New Science of Gratitude Can Make You Happier" says that gratitude is an attitude that can be chosen and cultivated with techniques such as keeping a gratitude journal, prayer, and using reminders to be thankful.

Being more thankful and appreciative has been shown to be one of the best ways to strengthen a marriage or any relationship and is also very important in parenting.

Putting the method into practice

"Praise God from whom all blessings flow."
From a hymn by Thomas Ken

Ponder the Infinite Eternal Almighty Divine Love that is God.

Do the Thank You Breath:
Breathe in deeply as you lift your heart and say to yourself, "Infinite Eternal God".

Sigh and exhale slowly as you whisper or silently say "Thank You, Thank You, Thank You, Thank You, Thank You, Thank You, Thank You, Thank You, Thank You, Thank You……" as many times as you can until you run out of breath.

Feel your heart beating and intend one "Thank You" for every heartbeat. This is literally heartfelt thanks and its power is difficult to overestimate.

Breathe in "Divine Love" as you lift your heart…and breathe out "Thank You, Thank You, Thank You, Thank You, Thank You, Thank You, Thank You, Thank You…"

Get in the habit of being more thankful.

Remember and give thanks to and for Infinite Eternal Omnipotent God/Divine Love.

Tell the people in your life that you appreciate them.

Appreciate yourself. Thank yourself for your contribution to the world. Be thankful that you are trying to be more thankful and that you are making an effort to tune in to God.

Keep a gratitude journal, writing at least five things per day for which you are thankful.

Be thankful for indoor plumbing and electricity and roads and the sun and so many things that we usually take for granted.

Give thanks for food and drink and everyone that helped it get to you before you eat or drink. Remember God/Divine Love when you eat and drink.

When you are driving down the road, think of some things/people that begin with the letter "A" that you are thankful for, then the letter "B", etc.

If you are adventurous, try being thankful for *all* things— even your challenges.

Give thanks in advance for blessings that are on their way and not yet apparent.

Remember that you are loved more than you can possibly comprehend. How can you not be thankful?

Remember to rejoice and be thankful.

Remember that Jesus gave thanks *before* the miracles occurred.

Try going through a day being thankful as often as you can. See what a challenge it is — how often you get distracted. That's why we need reminders.

"If the only prayer you ever say is thank you, that would be sufficient."

Meister Johann Eckhardt

Method #5

Tune in to God by looking up

In studying the miracles surrounding Jesus it is interesting that he often looked up just prior to a miracle occurring.

"Then they took away the stone from the place where the dead was laid. And Jesus lifted up his eyes, and said, Father, I thank thee that thou hast heard me. And I knew that thou hearest me always: but because of the people which stand by I said it, that they may believe that thou hast sent me. And when he thus had spoken, he cried with a loud voice, Lazarus, come forth. And he that was dead came forth..."

John 11:41-44

"And looking up to heaven, he sighed, and saith unto him, Ephphatha, that is, Be opened. And straightway his ears were opened, and the string of his tongue was loosed, and he spake plain."

Mark 7:34-35

"Then he took the five loaves and the two fishes, and looking up to heaven, he blessed them, and brake, and gave to the disciples to set before the multitude. And they did eat, and were all filled: and there was taken up of fragments that remained to them twelve baskets."

Luke 9:16

He also looked up at other times when he prayed.

"These words spake Jesus, and lifted up his eyes to heaven, and said, Father, the hour is come; glorify thy Son, that thy Son also may glorify thee..."

John 17:1

He also instructed his disciples to look up.

"...behold, I say unto you, Lift up your eyes, and look on the fields; for they are white already to harvest."
John 4:35

And when these things begin to come to pass, then look up, and lift up your heads; for your redemption draweth nigh.
Luke 21:28

So, maybe looking up is a method of tuning into God.

We were never taught this in Sunday School, but have been practicing it of late. Maybe it's the placebo effect, but knowing that Jesus used this method helps us to believe that the method is worthwhile and this believing helps even more to feel tuned in to God. There are other passages in the Bible that support the notion that looking up, lifting your eyes, gazing upward may be worth trying.

"And at the end of the days I Nebuchadnezzar lifted up mine eyes unto heaven, and mine understanding returned unto me, and I blessed the most High, and I praised and honoured him that liveth for ever, whose dominion is an everlasting dominion, and his kingdom is from generation to generation..."
Daniel 4:34

"Set your affection on things above, not on things on the earth."
Colossians 3:2

"Every good gift and every perfect gift is from above, and cometh down from the Father of lights, with whom is no variableness, neither shadow of turning."
James 1:17

"But he, being full of the Holy Ghost, looked up steadfastly into heaven, and saw the glory of God, and Jesus standing on the right hand of God,"
Acts 7:55 (referring to Stephen)

"And David lifted up his eyes, and saw the angel of the LORD stand between the earth and the heaven, having a drawn sword in his hand stretched out over Jerusalem. Then David and the elders of Israel, who were clothed in sackcloth, fell upon their faces."

1 Chronicles 21:16

"Lift up your eyes on high, and behold who hath created these things, that bringeth out their host by number: he calleth them all by names by the greatness of his might, for that he is strong in power: not one faileth."

Isaiah 40:26

"And while they looked steadfastly toward heaven as he went up, behold, two men stood by them in white apparel; Which also said, Ye men of Galilee, why stand ye gazing up into heaven? this same Jesus, which is taken up from you into heaven, shall so come in like manner as ye have seen him go into heaven."

Acts 1:10-11

"My voice shalt thou hear in the morning, O LORD; in the morning will I direct my prayer unto thee, and will look up."

Psalm 5:3

"And, behold, I send the promise of my Father upon you: but tarry ye in the city of Jerusalem, until ye be endued with power from on high."

Luke 24:49

I will lift up mine eyes unto the hills, from whence cometh my help. My help cometh from the LORD, which made heaven and earth.

Psalm 121:1-2

Unto thee lift I up mine eyes, O thou that dwellest in the heavens. Behold, as the eyes of servants look unto the hand of their masters, and as the eyes of a maiden unto the hand of her mistress; so our eyes wait upon the LORD our God, until that he have mercy upon us.

Psalm 123:1-2

"While we look not at the things which are seen, but at the things which are not seen: for the things which are seen are temporal; but the things which are not seen are eternal."
2 Corinthians 4:18

"And I, if I be lifted up from the earth, will draw all men unto me."
John 12:32

Jesus said,
"But seek ye first the kingdom of God, and his righteousness; and all these things shall be added unto you."
Matthew 6:33

And if we had to guess, the direction in which we would seek for the kingdom of God would be upward and inward.

"Neither shall they say, Lo here! or, lo there! for, behold, the kingdom of God is within you."
Luke 17:21

In many paintings of biblical characters and saints, they are depicted with their eyes looking upward.

So let us close our eyes and gaze upward. First, just close your eyes and let your eye muscles relax. The eye muscles are among the most used muscles in your body and among the most neglected. Just relax and be aware of your eyes. Now with your eyes still closed, without straining, lift your eyes so that you are gazing upward. That's all there is to it. Just watch, and listen, and observe.

"The light of the body is the eye: therefore when thine eye is single, thy whole body also is full of light; but when thine eye is evil, thy body also is full of darkness. Take heed therefore that the light which is in thee be not darkness. If thy whole body therefore be full of light, having no part dark, the whole shall be full of light, as when the bright shining of a candle doth give thee light."
Luke 11:34-36

Don't overdo this gazing upward.

After practicing this method for a while many people feel a sensation in their forehead. Some see patterns of light. Some feel a tingle at the top of their head (tongues of fire?). Some experience nothing out of the ordinary. There are no wrong or right experiences. Just play around with this method and see what, if anything, happens. Remember, the goal is to tune in to God, to seek first the Kingdom of Heaven. If you believe this method helps in that goal, it just might. Combining this method with some of the other methods definitely seems to help in the effort to tune in to God.

Validation from modern science

Some studies have shown that gazing upward stimulates the parasympathetic nervous system which lowers blood pressure and slows breathing.

Brain research and therapy techniques such as EMDR (Eye Movement Desensitization and Reprocessing), Eye Movement Therapy, NLP (NeuroLinguistic Programming), and EFT (Emotional Freedom Technique) have demonstrated that the direction in which your eyes move and are directed affects memory and emotion.

Whether we are stimulating our frontal lobe, clicking our amygdala, accessing memories, or activating our pineal gland does not matter. What matters is that Jesus did it and it works to help tune in to God.

"Looking up" is a colloquialism for being optimistic and Martin Seligman and others have done extensive research showing that optimists are healthier, happier, live longer, and are more successful.

Keep looking up!

He that dwelleth in the secret place of the most High shall abide under the shadow of the Almighty.

Psalm 91:1

Putting the method into practice

Close your eyes and gaze upward. Don't strain your eye muscles — just gently gaze upward. Just observe your experience. Not for too long — maybe just a minute or two to start. Then allow your eyes to relax.

Give thanks to the All-Powerful Eternal Infinite Omniscient Unconditional Love and Light that is the Creator.

Breathe deeply and sigh a few times.
Feel your heart beating.
Feel God's Love in your heart.

Look up, sigh and say "Ephphatha" which means "be opened". Jesus did this and a miracle occurred (Mark 7:34). You can be asking for your eyes to be opened to God's Kingdom or for the gates of heaven to be opened or for whatever you wish to have opened.

Breathe in, feeling your heart lifting and your gaze lifting and your awareness lifting.
Sigh and breathe out slowly and feel God's Love pulsing through your heart out to the world.

Repeat, with your eyes gazing upward and intending "God is" on the inhale and "Love, Love, Love, Love, Love, Love…………." on the exhale.

Repeat, gazing upward and intending "I am" on the inhale and "Love, Love, Love, Love, Love, Love, Love………..." on the exhale.

Place this book cover or one of our postcards with the radiant heart image in a position where you are gazing upward at it. Gaze for awhile while feeling your heart then close your eyes and see if you see an afterimage.

Remember you are loved more than you can possibly fathom and keep looking up!

Method #6

Tune in to God by smiling

If you have been playing along with the previous methods — pondering God, feeling His Love in your heart, looking up, and being thankful then there should have been some smiling going on.

And smiling helps even more to tune in to God.

While the scriptures do not explicitly report that Jesus gave instructions to smile, they do document His teachings that we are to rejoice and feel great joy and give thanks that the Kingdom is at hand and that we are to have life more abundantly. If we follow His teachings and apply His methods, how can we not smile?

"These things have I spoken unto you, that my joy might remain in you, and that your joy might be full."

John 15:11

"Rejoice ye in that day, and leap for joy: for, behold, your reward is great in heaven…"

Luke 6:23

"In that hour Jesus rejoiced in spirit, and said, I thank thee, O Father, Lord of heaven and earth, that thou hast hid these things from the wise and prudent, and hast revealed them unto babes: even so, Father; for so it seemed good in thy sight."

Luke 10:21

"...I am come that they might have life, and that they might have it more abundantly."

John 10:10

"And the seventy returned again with joy, saying, Lord, even the devils are subject unto us through thy name."

Luke 10:17

"...but be of good cheer; I have overcome the world."

John 16:33

"...rejoice, because your names are written in heaven."

Luke 10:20

A smile is an outward and visible sign of joy within. And the act of smiling can spread and increase joy.

Smiling is so important. It helps to tune in to Divinity. Your smile is like a radar dish helping you to tune in to God.

Many other Bible verses remind us and help us to feel joyful and smile.

"But let all those that put their trust in thee rejoice: let them ever shout for joy, because thou defendest them: let them also that love thy name be joyful in thee."

Psalm 5:11

"Now the God of hope fill you with all joy and peace in believing, that ye may abound in hope, through the power of the Holy Ghost."

Romans 15:13

"Thou hast put gladness in my heart, more than in the time that their corn and their wine increased."

Psalm 4:7

"But I have trusted in thy mercy; my heart shall rejoice in thy salvation."

Psalm 13:5

The LORD bless thee, and keep thee:
The LORD make his face shine upon thee, and be gracious unto thee:
The LORD lift up his countenance upon thee, and give thee peace.
Numbers 6:24-26

"*Turn us again, O God, and cause thy face to shine; and we shall be saved."*
Psalm 80:3

"*Rejoice in the Lord alway: and again I say, Rejoice."*
Philippians 4:4

"*Make thy face to shine upon thy servant; and teach me thy statutes."*
Psalm 119:135

And many other wise people through the ages have reminded us of the importance and power of the smile.

"Peace begins with a smile."
Mother Teresa of Calcutta

"True holiness consists of doing God's will with a smile."
Mother Teresa of Calcutta

"Smiling is very important. If we are not able to smile, then the world will not have peace. It is not by going out for a demonstration against nuclear missiles that we can bring about peace. It is with our capacity of smiling, breathing, and being peace that we can make peace."
Thich Nhat Hanh

"What sunshine is to flowers, smiles are to humanity. These are but trifles, to be sure; but, scattered along life's pathway, the good they do is inconceivable."

Joseph Addison

"If someone is too tired to give you a smile, leave one of your own, because no one needs a smile as much as those who have none to give."

Rabbi Samson Raphael Hirsch

"A smile is the easiest way to spread love and light and healing. The ripple effects of just one heartfelt smile are incalculable."
Suzie Ward

"Smile at each other, smile at your wife, smile at your husband, smile at your children, smile at each other — it doesn't matter who it is — and that will help you to grow up in greater love for each other."
Mother Teresa of Calcutta

Validation from modern science

The act of smiling has been shown in scientific research to:

- Change your mood in the direction of being happier
- Release endorphins which are natural painkillers
- Make you appear more attractive to others
- Make you more likely to receive help from others
- Boost the immune system and make you less likely to get sick
- Lower your blood pressure
- Increase customer satisfaction ratings
- Make you appear more confident and therefore more likely to be promoted
- Contribute to marriage stability and longer life expectancy
- Be contagious

"We don't smile because we are happy. We are happy because we smile."
William James

Even if you don't feel the joy within that produces a smile, fake it 'til you make it and your smile will help to produce the joy within.

Putting the method into practice

Remind yourself to smile.

Keep pictures around of loved ones smiling—that will make you smile.

Get in the habit of smiling at yourself in the mirror. Watch comedies. Remember happy memories. Keep a gratitude journal. Put a big ol' grit-eating grin on your face right now (we love our grits in the South).

Breathe deeply and sigh a sigh of relief that God is in charge.

Feel your heart beating.

Look up and give thanks to the All-Powerful Eternal Infinite Omniscient Unconditional Love that is your Father in Heaven. Smile.

As you breathe in deeply, feel your heart and your eyes and the corners of your mouth being lifted.

As you sigh and breathe out, smile and feel Divine Love flowing, pulsing, shining through your heart. Breathe in "I am". Breathe out "Love, Love, Love, Love, Love, Love, Love, Love, Love, Love….. Repeat. Feel God's Love in your heart and smile even bigger. Just rest in this feeling of joy and Love. Now you are tuned in to God.

Remember you are loved more than the human mind can conceive of……. and smile.

Method #7

Tune in to God by sending Love

If you have been practicing the preceding methods and tuning in to God then Divine Love is being sent through you. When you feel your heart and invite Divine Love into your heart and allow the blockages to be shined away then Divine Love flows through you. You realize that without even trying you are fulfilling the two great commandments. You are loving God with all your heart, soul, mind, and strength and loving your neighbor as yourself.

"And Jesus answered him, The first of all the commandments is, Hear, O Israel; The Lord our God is one Lord: And thou shalt love the Lord thy God with all thy heart, and with all thy soul, and with all thy mind, and with all thy strength: this is the first commandment. And the second is like, namely this, Thou shalt love thy neighbour as thyself. There is none other commandment greater than these."

Mark 12:29-31

As this Love shines through you in all directions you are loving your enemies and praying for those that persecute you.

"Ye have heard that it hath been said, Thou shalt love thy neighbour, and hate thine enemy. But I say unto you, Love your enemies, bless them that curse you, do good to them that hate you, and pray for them which despitefully use you, and persecute you; That ye may be the children of your Father which is in heaven: for he maketh his sun to rise on the evil and on the good, and sendeth rain on the just and on the unjust. For if ye love them which love you, what reward have ye? do not even the publicans the same? And if ye salute your brethren only, what do ye more than others? do not even the publicans so? Be ye therefore perfect, even as your Father which is in heaven is perfect."

Matthew 5:43-48

And you are also loving yourself. In order for God's Love to flow through you and bless the world, that Love has to touch and bless you first.

"Love cures people — both the ones who give it and the ones who receive it."
Karl A. Menninger, M.D.

Jesus' life was about sending Love. Jesus was the epitome of sending Love. His entire existence was about Love.

"For God so loved the world, that he gave his only begotten Son, that whosoever believeth in him should not perish, but have everlasting life."
John 3:16

Jesus sent Love by healing. Let us send Love by helping others, praying for others, and reminding ourselves and others to be healthy.

Jesus sent Love by feeding others. Let us send Love by feeding others. Bless your food and drinks and put Love into the food you prepare.

Jesus sent Love by serving. He washed His disciples' feet and taught that we should serve others. Let us help others.

"But he that is greatest among you shall be your servant. And whosoever shall exalt himself shall be abased; and he that shall humble himself shall be exalted."
Matthew 23:11-12

But Jesus did not take credit for these actions.

"I can of mine own self do nothing: as I hear, I judge: and my judgment is just; because I seek not mine own will, but the will of the Father which hath sent me."
John 5:30

A great way to send Love is to give anonymously. Give with no thought of being thanked, no thought of being recognized, no thought of a tax deduction.

"Take heed that ye do not your alms before men, to be seen of them: otherwise ye have no reward of your Father which is in heaven. Therefore when thou doest thine alms, do not sound a trumpet before thee, as the hypocrites do in the synagogues and in the streets, that they may have glory of men. Verily I say unto you, They have their reward. But when thou doest alms, let not thy left hand know what thy right hand doeth: That thine alms may be in secret: and thy Father which seeth in secret himself shall reward thee openly."

Matthew 6:1-4

"I have shewed you all things, how that so labouring ye ought to support the weak, and to remember the words of the Lord Jesus, how he said, It is more blessed to give than to receive."

Acts 20:35

Donate anonymously. Send anonymous postcards. Send a book or CD to someone anonymously. There are some more ideas on our website: *TuneintoGod.com*. Receiving an anonymous card or gift gives one a wonderful feeling and giving anonymously is an even more blessed experience. You may have received this book anonymously. Consider giving this book to others. Giving someone the gift of helping them tune in to God is a wonderful thing. Blessing and praying for others without telling anyone is another wonderful way to serve and give anonymously.

"Never answer an anonymous letter."

Yogi Berra

Jesus taught people that God is Love and His only commandment was to Love. Sending Love is one of the best ways to tune in to God.

"A new commandment I give unto you, That ye love one another; as I have loved you, that ye also love one another."
John 13:34

It is kind of like priming a pump. Sending Love starts the flow. Especially as you incorporate the other miracle methods of Jesus – as you ponder the attributes of God, sigh, smile, look up, and give heartfelt thanks – Divine Love flows through you. And let the miracles commence!

Send Love. Do random acts of kindness. Be creative – think of some new, fun ways to send Love. Send lots of Love, cheerfully, from your heart.

But this I say, He which soweth sparingly shall reap also sparingly; and he which soweth bountifully shall reap also bountifully. Every man according as he purposeth in his heart, so let him give; not grudgingly, or of necessity: for God loveth a cheerful giver. And God is able to make all grace abound toward you; that ye, always having all sufficiency in all things, may abound to every good work:
2 Corinthians 9:6-8

Other passages in the Bible also remind us of the value and importance of sending Love.

"My little children, let us not love in word, neither in tongue; but in deed and in truth."
1 John 3:18

"Let all that you do be done in love."
1 Corinthians 16:14 (English Standard Version)

"Above all, love each other deeply, because love covers over a multitude of sins."
1 Peter 4:8 (New International Version)

"Let your light so shine before men, that they may see your good works, and glorify your Father which is in heaven."

Matthew 5:16

"Let brotherly love continue. Be not forgetful to entertain strangers: for thereby some have entertained angels unawares."

Hebrews 13:1-2

Other folks widely considered to be wise have also reminded us to send Love.

"The heart that loves is forever young."

Greek proverb

"God doesn't look at how much we do, but with how much love we do it."

Mother Teresa of Calcutta

"You learn to speak by speaking, to study by studying, to run by running, to work by working; in just the same way, you learn to love by loving."

Anatole France

"No act of kindness, no matter how small, is ever wasted."

Aesop

"My bounty is as boundless as the sea, my love as deep; the more I give to thee, the more I have, for both are infinite."

William Shakespeare, from "Romeo and Juliet"

"Let us not be satisfied with just giving money. Money is not enough, money can be got, but they need your hearts to love them. So, spread your love everywhere you go."

Mother Teresa of Calcutta

"Nirvana or lasting enlightenment or true spiritual growth can be achieved only through persistent exercise of real love."

M. Scott Peck, M.D.

"Love is not automatic. It takes conscious practice and awareness, just like playing the piano or golf. However, you have ample opportunities to practice. Everyone you meet can be your practice session."
Doc Childre and Sara Paddison, HeartMath Discovery Program

"Spread love everywhere you go: first of all in your own house. Give love to your children, to your wife or husband, to a next door neighbor… Let no one ever come to you without leaving better or happier. Be the living expression of God's kindness; kindness in your face, kindness in your eyes, kindness in your smile; kindness in your warm greeting."
Mother Teresa of Calcutta

"Love is the cure, for your pain will keep giving birth to more pain until your eyes constantly exhale love as effortlessly as your body yields its scent."
Rumi

When you are tuned in to God sending Love is a natural consequence. God's Love will flow through you. And purposefully sending Love is a way to tune in to God.

Validation from modern science

Dr. Dean Ornish, M.D. has done extensive research with heart disease patients showing that the best predictor of longevity – more important than exercise, diet, and even quitting smoking is having close, intimate relationships.

People who volunteer and help others have been found to be healthier and live longer than those who don't. People who have pets are healthier and live longer. Nursing home residents given a plant to take care of live longer.

From data collected over decades of research many, many people who have had near-death experiences report that when they encountered the great, ineffable, Love-Light that most call God the only questions they felt that they were asked were, "How did you Love?" and "What did you learn about Love?" Let us prepare for our "final exam" at least a little bit today by sending Love in some fashion.

"By this shall all men know that ye are my disciples, if ye have love one to another."

John 13:35

Putting the method into practice

Send Love.

Pray for others.

Donate — your time, your money, books, and possessions — whatever you can give with a cheerful heart. Send anonymous cards, gifts, books, CDs.

Volunteer.

Hug.

Care for a pet or a plant.

Prepare food with Love.

Bless your food and drink.

Love and take care of yourself.

Bless yourself.

Bless others.

Smile.

Imagine a beautiful light (you choose the color) shining out of your heart, sending Love to people, trees, the sun, the earth, et al.

Send Love to God. Praise God! Thank God.

Whatever you do, try to do it with Love.

Remember a time when you loved unconditionally, not thinking of getting anything in return—maybe while holding a baby or a pet, or while spending time with a friend or a lover or someone who was dying.

Remember a time when you felt loved. Now multiply that by one thousand. And multiply that feeling again by one thousand. The Love that the Infinite All-Powerful God has for you is infinitely more than that.

Sigh and feel some heart-felt thanks.

Look up and give thanks to the Infinite Omnipotent Loving Father.

Smile and sigh a sigh of relief and joy that God is on the scene. Sigh again and feel your heart beating. Imagine a bright, dazzling light shining from your heart region.

Intend "I am" as you breathe in and feel your heart, your eyes, and the corners of your mouth lifting.
Intend "Sending Love" as you sigh and exhale slowly, feeling your heart pulsing out Love in all directions.

Smile bigger.

Do the Two Greatest Commandments Breath:

Intend "I Love God with all of my heart, soul, mind, and strength" as you inhale and feel lifted up.

Intend "I Love my neighbor as myself" as you sigh and exhale and feel Love flowing and shining from your heart in all directions. And exhale more completely.

Repeat as needed.

Remember you are loved more than you can conceive of. Sending Love tunes you in to God/Divine Love and then this current of Divine Love flows through you even more.

Method #8

Tune in to God by forgiving

Jesus was big on forgiveness. Many of us are out of tune with God to some degree because of lack of forgiveness.

Many of Jesus' teachings, parables, and actions were instructions on forgiveness. He taught that forgiveness is a prerequisite to our being forgiven and to having our prayers answered.

"And forgive us our debts, as we forgive our debtors. And lead us not into temptation, but deliver us from evil: For thine is the kingdom, and the power, and the glory, for ever. Amen. For if ye forgive men their trespasses, your heavenly Father will also forgive you: But if ye forgive not men their trespasses, neither will your Father forgive your trespasses."
Matthew 6:12-15

"Then came Peter to him, and said, Lord, how oft shall my brother sin against me, and I forgive him? till seven times? Jesus saith unto him, I say not unto thee, Until seven times: but, Until seventy times seven."
Matthew 18:21-22

"And when ye stand praying, forgive, if ye have ought against any: that your Father also which is in heaven may forgive you your trespasses. But if ye do not forgive, neither will your Father which is in heaven forgive your trespasses."
Mark 11:25-26

"So likewise shall my heavenly Father do also unto you, if ye from your hearts forgive not every one his brother their trespasses."
Matthew 18:35

"Judge not, and ye shall not be judged: condemn not, and ye shall not be condemned: forgive, and ye shall be forgiven: Give, and it shall be given unto you; good measure, pressed down, and shaken together, and running over, shall men give into your bosom. For with the same measure that ye mete withal it shall be measured to you again."
Luke 6:37-38

Forgiveness is a natural, logical consequence of trying to follow the Golden Rule that is found in all of the world's major religions. We have all erred and would like to be forgiven.

"Therefore all things whatsoever ye would that men should do to you, do ye even so to them: for this is the law and the prophets."
Matthew 7:12

But forgiveness is not always easy. Sometimes it takes some work. Sometimes we might need to appropriately express some feelings of anger before we can forgive.

"Be ye angry, and sin not: let not the sun go down upon your wrath…"
Ephesians 4:26

Anger is a normal human emotion and keeping feelings of anger inside or pretending like these feelings aren't there is not healthy. Acknowledging feelings of anger can be a step in the process of forgiveness. It is normal to get angry when you get hurt or when you see injustice. Jesus got angry.

"And they come to Jerusalem: and Jesus went into the temple, and began to cast out them that sold and bought in the temple, and overthrew the tables of the moneychangers, and the seats of them that sold doves; And would not suffer that any man should carry any vessel through the temple. And he taught, saying unto them, Is it not written, My house shall be called of all nations the house of prayer? but ye have made it a den of thieves."
Mark 11:15-17

Sometimes we may need to forgive God. Not that God needs our forgiveness, but it is very common for people to get angry at God when something happens that they cannot understand or accept.

Again, getting the feelings of anger out in an appropriate way is sometimes called for before forgiveness can occur.

Talk about it. Pray about it. Write a letter to God expressing the feelings of anger. It's okay—God can take it.

The danger for some is keeping these feelings inside because they feel guilty for feeling angry at God or they feel afraid that God will smite them if they are angry at God. Some of these people end up distancing themselves from God and this is definitely not healthy.

Sometimes the most difficult part of forgiveness is forgiving your self. Many of us tend to be harder on ourselves than we are on others. Many of us carry around guilt that weighs us down and prevents us from tuning in to God and letting His Light and Love shine through us.

While we should be heartily sorry for our mistakes and strive to not repeat them, beating our self up is not a very loving thing to do.

Jesus reminded people again and again that if they repented and asked for forgiveness that they were forgiven.

"When Jesus saw their faith, he said unto the sick of the palsy, Son, thy sins be forgiven thee."

Mark 2:5

In the Aramaic language that Jesus spoke the word "forgive" means to "untie".

Forgiveness is not about condoning or doing a favor for the other person. Forgiveness is about taking care of our self and letting go of the chains that bind us to bitterness and resentment so that we may enter the Kingdom—so that we can tune in to God.

Don't feel guilty or not good enough if you are not ready to forgive. For many of us forgiveness is a process that takes time and sometimes assistance from a counselor, pastor, mentor, or other source. If you continue to practice the other methods of Jesus, you will eventually be able to forgive.

Other passages in the Bible remind us of the importance and availability of forgiveness.

"And be ye kind one to another, tenderhearted, forgiving one another, even as God for Christ's sake hath forgiven you."
Ephesians 4:32

"The discretion of a man deferreth his anger; and it is his glory to pass over a transgression."
Proverbs 19:11

"Forbearing one another, and forgiving one another, if any man have a quarrel against any: even as Christ forgave you, so also do ye."
Colossians 3:13

"Seek ye the LORD while he may be found, call ye upon him while he is near: Let the wicked forsake his way, and the unrighteous man his thoughts: and let him return unto the LORD, and he will have mercy upon him; and to our God, for he will abundantly pardon."
Isaiah 55:6-7

"For thou, Lord, art good, and ready to forgive; and plenteous in mercy unto all them that call upon thee."
Psalm 86:5

"Repent ye therefore, and be converted, that your sins may be blotted out, when the times of refreshing shall come from the presence of the Lord;"

Acts 3:19

"Who is a God like unto thee, that pardoneth iniquity, and passeth by the transgression of the remnant of his heritage? He retaineth not his anger for ever, because he delighteth in mercy. He will turn again, he will have compassion upon us; he will subdue our iniquities; and thou wilt cast all their sins into the depths of the sea."

Micah 7:18-19

Other wise people have also realized and reminded us of the value and importance of forgiveness.

"Forgiveness is choosing to love. It is the first skill of self-giving love."

Mahatma Gandhi

"We must develop and maintain the capacity to forgive. He who is devoid of the power to forgive is devoid of the power to love. There is some good in the worst of us and some evil in the best of us. When we discover this, we are less prone to hate our enemies."

Martin Luther King, Jr.

"To err is human; to forgive, divine."

Alexander Pope

"Always forgive your enemies — nothing annoys them so much."

Oscar Wilde

"The weak can never forgive. Forgiveness is the attribute of the strong."

Mahatma Gandhi

If you have been trying the methods from the previous chapters you are being forgiving without even really trying. When you open and cleanse your heart and send Love, forgiveness just happens. When you sigh and let go and let God you are letting go of the past and enjoying and appreciating the Infinite Divine Love that is now and forever.

Sometimes it helps to just realize that some people were not as fortunate as some of us were to be brought up in loving families. Some people just weren't raised right.

"Then said Jesus, Father, forgive them; for they know not what they do."
Luke 23:34

Even if you weren't raised right, it's never too late to learn. And even if you were raised right, we still forget and need reminders.

A Note to Parents: You can be the best parent and raise your child right and they still may stray. Just keep sending Love.

Validation from modern science

A Campaign for Forgiveness Research is an organization that funds scientific research on forgiveness. Several studies have shown evidence that forgiveness can be learned and that forgiving results in improved physical and mental health.

"Forgiveness is both a decision and a real change in emotional experience. That change in emotion is related to better mental and physical health."
Everett L. Worthington, Jr., PhD., Executive Director of A Campaign for Forgiveness Research

Putting the method into practice

Relax and take a few deeper breaths.

Say aloud, "I release and forgive everyone who ever hurt me to the best of my ability and I ask God to help me be more forgiving".

Breathe deeply and sigh and gaze upward.

Say aloud, "I am heartily sorry for any harm I have done to others and myself. I ask for forgiveness and accept forgiveness for myself. I totally love and accept and forgive myself."

Breathe deeply and sigh a sigh of relief that you have forgiven others and that you are forgiven.

Give heartfelt thanks with a Thank You Breath.

Remembering that you are loved more than you have the capability to comprehend helps you to forgive others and yourself.

Method #9

Tune in to God by asking and believing

Let us remember that our goal is to tune in to God. And let us remember that God is Spirit.

"God is a Spirit: and they that worship him must worship him in spirit and in truth."

John 4:24

And God is Love.

"He that loveth not knoweth not God; for God is love."

1 John 4:8

Where a lot of us have gotten confused (the authors included) is being focused on physical things instead of the spiritual.

It seems that Jesus was trying to get people to not focus so much on this physical world and was directing people to tune in to and seek the Kingdom of Heaven, the Kingdom of God, the spiritual world.

"Therefore I say unto you, Take no thought for your life, what ye shall eat, or what ye shall drink; nor yet for your body, what ye shall put on. Is not the life more than meat, and the body than raiment? Behold the fowls of the air: for they sow not, neither do they reap, nor gather into barns; yet your heavenly Father feedeth them. Are ye not much better than they? Which of you by taking thought can add one cubit unto his stature? And why take ye thought for raiment? Consider the lilies of the field, how they grow; they toil not, neither do they spin: And yet I say unto you, That even Solomon in all his glory was not arrayed like one of these. Wherefore, if God so clothe the

grass of the field, which today is, and tomorrow is cast into the oven, shall he not much more clothe you, O ye of little faith? Therefore take no thought, saying, What shall we eat? or, What shall we drink? or, Wherewithal shall we be clothed? (For after all these things do the Gentiles seek:) for your heavenly Father knoweth that ye have need of all these things. But seek ye first the kingdom of God, and his righteousness; and all these things shall be added unto you."

Matthew 6:25-33

So let us ask for things spiritual. If we tune in to Spirit/God all "these things" will be added. Leave the specifics up to God.

"If ye then be risen with Christ, seek those things which are above, where Christ sitteth on the right hand of God. Set your affection on things above, not on things on the earth."

Colossians 3:1-2

"For the kingdom of God is not meat and drink; but righteousness, and peace, and joy in the Holy Ghost."

Romans 14:17

"For he that soweth to his flesh shall of the flesh reap corruption; but he that soweth to the Spirit shall of the Spirit reap life everlasting."

Galatians 6:8

Even Jesus, when he asked for specific physical outcomes, did not always get what he asked for.

"And he went forward a little, and fell on the ground, and prayed that, if it were possible, the hour might pass from him. And he said, Abba, Father, all things are possible unto thee; take away this cup from me: nevertheless not what I will, but what thou wilt."

Mark 14:35-36

So let us ask for Love.

"Pursue love, and desire spiritual gifts, but especially the gift of speaking what God has revealed."

1 Corinthians 14:1 (God's Word Translation)

Let us ask for wisdom as Solomon did.

"Give therefore thy servant an understanding heart to judge thy people, that I may discern between good and bad: for who is able to judge this thy so great a people? And the speech pleased the Lord, that Solomon had asked this thing. And God said unto him, Because thou hast asked this thing, and hast not asked for thyself long life; neither hast asked riches for thyself, nor hast asked the life of thine enemies; but hast asked for thyself understanding to discern judgment; Behold, I have done according to thy words: lo, I have given thee a wise and an understanding heart; so that there was none like thee before thee, neither after thee shall any arise like unto thee. And I have also given thee that which thou hast not asked, both riches, and honour: so that there shall not be any among the kings like unto thee all thy days. And if thou wilt walk in my ways, to keep my statutes and my commandments, as thy father David did walk, then I will lengthen thy days."

1 Kings 3:9-14

"If any of you lack wisdom, let him ask of God, that giveth to all men liberally, and upbraideth not; and it shall be given him."

James 1:5

Let us ask for peace.

"And let the peace of God rule in your hearts, to which also ye are called in one body; and be ye thankful."

Colossians 3:15

"Let us therefore follow after the things which make for peace…"

Romans 14:19

Let us ask for joy.

"As the Father hath loved me, so have I loved you: continue ye in my love. If ye keep my commandments, ye shall abide in my love; even as I have kept my Father's commandments, and abide in his love. These things have I spoken unto you, that my joy might remain in you, and that your joy might be full."

John 15:9-11

Let us ask for awareness of the Kingdom of God.

"And seek not ye what ye shall eat, or what ye shall drink, neither be ye of doubtful mind. For all these things do the nations of the world seek after: and your Father knoweth that ye have need of these things. But rather seek ye the kingdom of God; and all these things shall be added unto you. Fear not, little flock; for it is your Father's good pleasure to give you the kingdom."

Luke 12: 29-32

Jesus instructed his followers to ask in His Name.

"And whatsoever ye shall ask in my name, that will I do, that the Father may be glorified in the Son. If ye shall ask any thing in my name, I will do it."

John 14:13-14

"Verily, verily, I say unto you, Whatsoever ye shall ask the Father in my name, he will give it you. Hitherto have ye asked nothing in my name: ask, and ye shall receive, that your joy may be full."

John 16:23-24

It seems that it is not so much about saying the name "Jesus" as it is tuning in to the spirit of Jesus, the vibration of Jesus, and tuning in to the spirit of God which is Divine Love.

"Abide in me, and I in you. As the branch cannot bear fruit of itself, except it abide in the vine; no more can ye, except ye abide in me. I am the vine, ye are the branches: He that abideth in me, and I in him, the same bringeth forth much fruit: for without me ye can do nothing. If a man abide not in me, he is cast forth as a branch, and is withered; and men gather them, and cast them into the fire, and they are burned. If ye abide in me, and my words abide in you, ye shall ask what ye will, and it shall be done unto you. Herein is my Father glorified, that ye bear much fruit; so shall ye be my disciples. As the Father hath loved me, so have I loved you: continue ye in my love. If ye keep my commandments, ye shall abide in my love; even as I have kept my Father's commandments, and abide in his love. These things have I

spoken unto you, that my joy might remain in you, and that your joy might be full."

John 15:4-11

It's about tuning in to God/Divine Love. Jesus was tuned in to God and His words and example show us how to do likewise. Someone should write a book about how to tune in to God. Oh, that's right, some people did. And you're reading it!

Another method that Jesus taught that goes along with asking is believing.

"Therefore I say unto you, What things soever ye desire, when ye pray, believe that ye receive them, and ye shall have them."

Mark 11:24

"Jesus answered and said unto them, Verily I say unto you, If ye have faith, and doubt not, ye shall not only do this which is done to the fig tree, but also if ye shall say unto this mountain, Be thou removed, and be thou cast into the sea; it shall be done. And all things, whatsoever ye shall ask in prayer, believing, ye shall receive."

Matthew 21:21-22

"And Jesus said unto him, Go thy way; thy faith hath made thee whole. And immediately he received his sight, and followed Jesus in the way."

Mark 10:52

So all we have to do is believe. But for most of us that is much easier said than done. So how do we believe? Contrary to a popular idiom, seeing is not believing.

"Now faith is the substance of things hoped for, the evidence of things not seen."

Hebrews 11:1

"Judge not according to the appearance, but judge righteous judgment."

John 7:24

In our experience believing has much more to do with the heart than with the eyes. And some of the earlier methods that help you to feel and appreciate and open and cleanse your heart will go a long way toward helping you believe and feel God's Love.

"For verily I say unto you, That whosoever shall say unto this mountain, Be thou removed, and be thou cast into the sea; and shall not doubt in his heart, but shall believe that those things which he saith shall come to pass; he shall have whatsoever he saith."
Mark 11:23

And let us give thanks that we have received that for which we have asked.

"Asking is the seed; the feeling of thanks is the water. God is the sunshine (Love and Light)."
The authors

And keep asking, keep knocking, keep seeking (first) the Kingdom of God and His righteousness.

"Ask, and it shall be given you; seek, and ye shall find; knock, and it shall be opened unto you: For every one that asketh receiveth; and he that seeketh findeth; and to him that knocketh it shall be opened. Or what man is there of you, whom if his son ask bread, will he give him a stone? Or if he ask a fish, will he give him a serpent? If ye then, being evil, know how to give good gifts unto your children, how much more shall your Father which is in heaven give good things to them that ask him?"
Matthew 7:7-11

Do the math. Infinity = Infinity. Omnipresence = Omnipresence.
If God is everywhere then He is here now and we just have to remember to tune in.

If we use Method #1 and remember that God is Infinite Eternal Omnipresent Divine Love then all we really have to ask for is the release of our blockages to God. Just relax and let go and let God and believe that God is here, now. Feeling God's Love in your heart helps you to believe that God is on the scene and in charge. Smile.

A very important key is to believe and feel in your heart the feeling of being loved and cared for. What does it feel like to have all of your needs met? Feel that feeling of peace and joy and gratitude. These miracle methods of Jesus help you to feel the Divine peace and joy and Love that Jesus lived and spoke of.

For with the heart man believeth unto righteousness; and with the mouth confession is made unto salvation.
Romans 10:10

If you do want to ask for a specific physical outcome just remember to make sure that "If it be Thy Will" or "Thy Will be done" is in there somewhere and be willing to surrender your wishes to God's Will (see the next chapter).

And remember to give thanks!

Validation from modern science

Decades of research on assertiveness have shown that people who are more assertive and ask for what they want are more happy, less depressed, and more successful than those less assertive.

Research on hypnosis and the placebo effect has shown that if one believes something to be true, it is true for them. For example, if a hypnotized subject is told and believes that a pencil eraser is a lit cigarette then if they are touched with the pencil eraser a blister will form as if they have been burned. And if a person is given a pill and believes that it will have a certain effect, much of the time that effect occurs even if the pill was a fake.

"Whether you think you can, or think you can't – you're right."
Henry Ford

Putting the method into practice

Think about how Great, Powerful, and Loving God is. Look up and sigh and smile and feel your heart. Any concern you may have – health, finances, relationships, or anything else – sigh and turn it over to God. Allow God/Divine Love to be in charge. As you tune in to God and ask for peace, joy, and Love in the Name, the vibration of Jesus, as you seek first the Kingdom of God – all of "these things" will be added unto you. Feel the joy in your heart that all of your needs are met. Feel some heartfelt thanks.

Say or intend: "Infinite Eternal Heavenly Father may I be tuned in to You better and better each day. I ask that Your Love, Peace, Wisdom, and Joy be manifest in my life according to Your Will." Look up, smile and sigh: "Thank You, Thank You, Thank You, Thank You, Thank You, Thank You, Thank You, that it is so." Relax and *feel* this to be so in your heart. Spend a few moments enjoying the feeling that God is in charge and all of your needs are met. If you are not smiling you are not doing it correctly.

Remember that you are loved more than you can imagine and feel thanks in your heart and believe that you are tuned in to God and His blessings.

Method #10

Tune in to God by surrendering to God

All of the preceding methods have been leading up to this point—total surrender to God.

We have been getting more and more tuned in to God. Now it is time to turn over the reins, to let go and let God, to allow Divine Love to be in charge.

The teachings of Jesus and His example over and over emphasize the importance of surrendering to God.

Jesus is the epitome of, the poster child for surrendering to God.

"I can of mine own self do nothing: as I hear, I judge: and my judgment is just; because I seek not mine own will, but the will of the Father which hath sent me."

John 5:30

"For I came down from heaven, not to do mine own will, but the will of him that sent me."

John 6:38

"And he said unto them, When ye pray, say, Our Father which art in heaven, Hallowed be thy name. Thy kingdom come. Thy will be done, as in heaven, so in earth."

Luke 11:2

"Saying, Father, if thou be willing, remove this cup from me: nevertheless not my will, but thine, be done."
Luke 22:42

"Jesus saith unto them, My meat is to do the will of him that sent me, and to finish his work."
John 4:34

"Not every one that saith unto me, Lord, Lord, shall enter into the kingdom of heaven; but he that doeth the will of my Father which is in heaven."
Matthew 7:21

And there are many other passages in the Bible that remind us to surrender our will to the Creator's Will.

"I delight to do thy will, O my God: yea, thy law is within my heart."
Psalm 40:8

"Humble yourselves in the sight of the Lord, and he shall lift you up."
James 4:10

"Teach me to do thy will; for thou art my God: thy spirit is good; lead me into the land of uprightness."
Psalm 143:10

Raising one's hands in the air is an act that signifies surrender in many cultures. Raise your hands high in the air like you are surrendering (to God). Breathe deeply and sigh – this allows air to better get into the upper part of the lungs and lifts and cleanses your heart.

"Let us lift up our heart with our hands unto God in the heavens."
Lamentations 3:41

"And he led them out as far as to Bethany, and he lifted his hands, and blessed them. And it came to pass, while he blessed them, he was parted from them, and carried up into heaven."
Luke 24:50-51

Getting down on one's knees is an act of submission and surrender that Jesus did.

"And he was withdrawn from them about a stone's cast, and kneeled down, and prayed,"
Luke 22:41

Bowing one's head is also an act of submission and surrender and is often associated with prayer. We have found that when thinking of God, sighing, smiling, being thankful, and gazing upward that bowing the head helps us to be more aware of our heart, more aware of Divine Love flowing through us.

Validation from modern science

One of the most effective systems for dealing with any type of addictive behavior and restoring people to sanity is the 12-Step program that was started with Alcoholics Anonymous. It also emphasizes surrender to God.

"Made a decision to turn our will and our lives over to the care of God as we understood him."
Step 3 of the 12 Steps

There has long been anecdotal evidence and now there is scientific support for the notion that giving up, surrendering, stopping trying can help one achieve some goals.

The tip-of-tongue phenomenon: When trying to remember a word or a name, sometimes the harder you keep trying makes it more difficult. Often when you stop trying and think about something else the desired word or name is remembered.

Many couples trying to conceive a child have found that when they stop trying, many times after deciding to adopt, that they do get pregnant.

Putting the method into practice

Look up and give thanks to the Infinite Eternal Loving Father. Breathe deeply and sigh a sigh of relief that God is in charge. Say "I surrender my will to the Creator's Will."

Lift your hands high, breathe deeply and sigh and surrender to God.

Get down on your knees every once in awhile (if you're sure you can get back up).

Do the God's Will Breath:
Breathe in allowing your heart, your eyes and your smile to be lifted up as you intend "Thy Will is done in Heaven." Sigh and breathe out slowly, bowing your head and feeling your heartbeat pulsing out Divine Love as you intend "Thy Will be done on earth." Repeat.

If you find yourself worrying about a situation, try to catch yourself before you worry too much. Look up, sigh, smile and remind yourself, "I surrender this situation to God." "I turn this over to God." "May God's Will be done."

Remember you are loved unconditionally and eternally, more than you can imagine. Relax and surrender to that Love.

Method #11

Tune in to God by remembering who you are

We have forgotten our true identity. Like the prodigal child we have wandered into a far country and become distracted and disconnected from our Father and our identity. The life and teachings of Jesus provide reminders and methods for us to repent, to turn, to tune in to God and thereby realize the Kingdom of Heaven. When we remember our Father and turn to Him and tune in to Him we are filled with joy and have life more abundantly.

It seems that the human condition is one of forgetfulness. As we say here in the South, we are "bad to forget". Peter recognized the human tendency to forget and saw one of his tasks as reminding others of the truth.

"Wherefore I will not be negligent to put you always in remembrance of these things, though ye know them, and be established in the present truth. Yea, I think it meet, as long as I am in this tabernacle, to stir you up by putting you in remembrance; Knowing that shortly I must put off this my tabernacle, even as our Lord Jesus Christ hath shewed me. Moreover I will endeavour that ye may be able after my decease to have these things always in remembrance."

2 Peter 1:12-15

By using the miracle methods of Jesus we can tune in to and feel our connection to God and remember who we really are. Reading or hearing passages like the following ones will help to remind you of who you really are.

"Ye are the light of the world. A city that is set on an hill cannot be hid. Neither do men light a candle, and put it under a bushel, but on a candlestick; and it giveth light unto all that are in the house. Let your light so shine before men, that they may see your good works, and glorify your Father which is in heaven."

Matthew 5:14-16

"We are not human beings having a spiritual experience. We are spiritual beings having a human experience."

Teilhard de Chardin

"Behold, what manner of love the Father hath bestowed upon us, that we should be called the sons of God…"

1 John 3:1

"But love ye your enemies, and do good, and lend, hoping for nothing again; and your reward shall be great, and ye shall be the children of the Highest…"

Luke 6:35

"Then shall the righteous shine forth as the sun in the kingdom of their Father. Who hath ears to hear, let him hear."

Matthew 13:43

"And they that be wise shall shine as the brightness of the firmament; and they that turn many to righteousness as the stars forever and ever."

Daniel 12:3

"When we've been there ten thousand years
Bright shining as the sun
We've no less days to sing God's praise
Than when we'd first begun."

From the hymn, "Amazing Grace"

"At that day ye shall know that I am in my Father, and ye in me, and I in you."

John 14:20

"Beloved, now are we the sons of God, and it doth not yet appear what we shall be: but we know that, when he shall appear, we shall be like him; for we shall see him as he is."

1 John 3:2

"When I consider thy heavens, the work of thy fingers, the moon and the stars, which thou hast ordained; What is man, that thou art mindful of him? and the son of man, that thou visitest him? For thou hast made him a little lower than the angels, and hast crowned him with glory and honour."

Psalm 8:3-5

"I can do all things through Christ which strengtheneth me."

Philippians 4:13

"Know ye that the LORD he is God: it is he that hath made us, and not we ourselves; we are his people, and the sheep of his pasture."

Psalm 100:3

"Every good gift and every perfect gift is from above, and cometh down from the Father of lights, with whom is no variableness, neither shadow of turning. Of his own will begat he us with the word of truth, that we should be a kind of first fruits of his creatures."

James 1:17-18

"Jesus answered them, Is it not written in your law, I said, Ye are gods? If he called them gods, unto whom the word of God came, and the scripture cannot be broken;"

John 10:34-35

"I have said, Ye are gods; and all of you are children of the most High."

Psalm 82:6

"And because ye are sons, God hath sent forth the Spirit of his Son into your hearts, crying, Abba, Father. Wherefore thou art no more a servant, but a son; and if a son, then an heir of God through Christ."

Galatians 4:6-7

"Ye are all the children of light, and the children of the day: we are not of the night, nor of darkness."

1 Thessalonians 5:5

"That they should seek the Lord, if haply they might feel after him, and find him, though he be not far from every one of us: For in him we live, and move, and have our being; as certain also of your own poets have said, For we are also his offspring. Forasmuch then as we are the offspring of God, we ought not to think that the Godhead is like unto gold, or silver, or stone, graven by art and man's device."

Acts 17:27-29

Remember whose child you are!

Validation from modern science

Research on amnesia has shown that frequent reminders help amnesiacs remember who they are and things they wish to remember.
In memory research one of the most powerful effects is repetition. What is repeated more often is more likely to be remembered later.
So keep reading, listening to, thinking, saying, and singing things that remind you of who you really are.

Putting the method into practice

Admit that you have amnesia—that you have forgotten who you really are.

Try to set aside some time on a regular basis to tune in to God, to remind yourself of your true identity and your relationship to God.

Read books like this one that remind you of your true identity.

Subscribe to the twice-weekly Tune In To God email reminder.

Do the "I Am Love Breath"

Breathe in, "I am"

Breathe out, "Love, Love, Love, Love, Love, Love, Love………"

Feel your breathing and your heartbeat.

Listen to <u>Tuning In To God: An audio guide to the miracle methods of Jesus.</u>

Do the "I am the Light Breath."

Inhale as you look upward and intend "I am the Light." And sigh and exhale as you intend "The Light I am."

Just tune in to God and allow God's Love and Light to shine through you. After all, Jesus said *let* your light shine, not *make* your light shine.

As the prodigal child who has wandered away and made mistakes, arise and turn (upward) toward your Father and ask, "May I please return to living in your kingdom?"

Use affirmations, prayers, and other methods listed in other chapters.

Remember whose child you are!

Remember that you are loved more than you can imagine and remind others that they are loved.

Method #12

Tune in to God with tunes

Music is a powerful tool that can help you to tune in to God. Jesus and His disciples certainly used this method. Music and song were very important to the culture and tradition in which Jesus was raised.

"And when they had sung an hymn, they went out into the mount of Olives."

Mark 14:26

Chanting, toning, whistling, and singing are great ways to tune in to God with tunes.

These methods also extend the exhale similar to the sigh and can help you to feel your heart.

"Make a joyful noise unto God, all ye lands: Sing forth the honour of his name: make his praise glorious."

Psalm 66:1-2

"Sing praises to God, sing praises: sing praises unto our King, sing praises. For God is the King of all the earth: sing ye praises with understanding."

Psalm 47:6-7

"Sing unto God, sing praises to his name: extol him that rideth upon the heavens by his name JAH, and rejoice before him."

Psalm 68:4

"Therefore I will give thanks unto thee, O LORD, among the heathen, and I will sing praises unto thy name."

2 Samuel 22:50

There are some songs and pieces of music that can help us to tune in to God. Everyone's taste is different. Here are a few songs that work for some of our group.

Gettin' In Tune by The Who
Blue Sky by the Allman Brothers
Shower the People You Love With Love by James Taylor
The Music Never Stopped by The Grateful Dead
Estimated Prophet by The Grateful Dead
Let It Be by the Beatles
Into the Mystic by Van Morrison
You Turn Me On, I'm a Radio by Joni Mitchell
Higher Love by Steve Winwood
All You Need Is Love by the Beatles
Oh Happy Day traditional hymn
How Great Thou Art traditional hymn
Amazing Grace traditional hymn
Let Your Love Flow by The Bellamy Brothers
Light of the World from Godspell
Morning Has Broken by Cat Stevens
The Hallelujah Chorus in Handel's *Messiah*
Here Comes the Sun by The Beatles
What a Wonderful World by Louis Armstrong
Time and a Word by Yes
Divine Intervention by Matthew Sweet
9th Symphony by Beethoven
Requiem by Mozart

(You can tell that some of us are old)
We would love to hear what works for you. Email your tunes that tune you in to God to tunes(at)TuneintoGod.com

Maybe make up your own song.

"I will sing a new song unto thee, O God: upon a psaltery and an instrument of ten strings will I sing praises unto thee."
Psalm 144:9

Many other people widely considered wise have extolled the benefits and wonders of music.

"Music is a moral law. It gives soul to the universe, wings to the mind, flight to the imagination, and charm and gaiety to life and to everything."
Plato

"Music takes us out of the actual and whispers to us dim secrets that startle our wonder as to who we are, and for what, whence, and whereto."
Ralph Waldo Emerson

"Music produces a kind of pleasure which human nature cannot do without."
Confucius

"Music and rhythm find their way into the secret places of the soul."
Plato

"Music is well said to be the speech of angels; in fact, nothing among the utterances allowed to man is felt to be so divine. It brings us near to the infinite."
Thomas Carlyle

"Music is the language of the spirit. It opens the secret of life bringing peace, abolishing strife."
Kahlil Gibran

"After silence, that which comes nearest to expressing the inexpressible is music."
Aldous Huxley

"Music and silence combine strongly because music is done with silence, and silence is full of music."

Marcel Marceau

"The aim and final end of all music should be none other than the glory of God and the refreshment of the soul."

Johann Sebastian Bach

Validation from modern science

Numerous scientific studies have shown the value of music. Music has been found to:
- decrease anxiety
- improve depressed mood
- help treat insomnia
- lower blood pressure
- enhance group cohesion
- help babies to grow faster and smarter
- reduce tension
- reduce headaches and chronic pain
- improve coordination

Putting the method into practice

Make a playlist of music that uplifts you, tunes you in to God. For some of us less techno-savvy folks, get your child or grandchild or other youngster to do it for you.

Sing, chant, tone, hum, whistle, play a musical instrument. Make a joyful noise unto the Lord. Woohoo!

Method #13

Tune in to God with nature

Jesus spent a lot of time in nature.

"And he withdrew himself into the wilderness, and prayed."

Luke 5:16

"And Jesus being full of the Holy Ghost returned from Jordan, and was led by the Spirit into the wilderness…"

Luke 4:1

And He spoke often of aspects of nature to help explain His teachings about God, His Kingdom, and our place in it.

"And why take ye thought for raiment? Consider the lilies of the field, how they grow; they toil not, neither do they spin: And yet I say unto you, That even Solomon in all his glory was not arrayed like one of these."

Matthew 6:28-29

"…for he maketh his sun to rise on the evil and on the good, and sendeth rain on the just and on the unjust."

Matthew 5:45

"But he answered and said, Every plant, which my heavenly Father hath not planted, shall be rooted up."

Matthew 15:13

He also spoke of animals to help illustrate the principles he was teaching.

"And he said unto them, What man shall there be among you, that shall have one sheep, and if it fall into a pit on the sabbath day, will he not lay hold on it, and lift it out? How much then is a man better than a sheep? Wherefore it is lawful to do well on the sabbath days."
Matthew 12:11-12

Several of Jesus' disciples were fishermen and it is mentioned several times how Jesus went out in a boat with his disciples. Boating and fishing are great ways to get in touch with nature and to tune in to God.

"There is certainly something in angling that tends to produce a serenity of the mind."
Washington Irving

"Give a man a fish and he has food for a day; teach him how to fish and you can get rid of him for the entire weekend."
Zenna Schaffer

"Three-fourths of the Earth's surface is water, and one-fourth is land. It is quite clear that the good Lord intended us to spend triple the amount of time fishing as taking care of the lawn."
Chuck Clark

Validation from modern science.

In the relatively new field of ecopsychology there is research showing the physical, mental, and spiritual benefits of being in and interacting with nature.

Many treatment centers, hospitals, and nursing homes use horticulture therapy, pet therapy and/or equine therapy to improve physical and emotional health.

Gardening has been shown as an effective treatment for depression.

The vitamin D your body produces from being in sunlight is essential for health.

Putting the method into practice

Go outside and breathe deeply the fresh air. Bask in the sun (in moderation).

Plant a plant. Take a walk in nature. Walk barefoot in the grass.

Give thanks for the sun, for oxygen producing plants, for animals and insects.

Pet a pet. Some pets can teach us about unconditional Love.

Stargaze. Gaze at clouds.

Look up, sigh, smile, feel your heart, and send Love to the earth.

"I love to think of nature as an unlimited broadcast station, through which God speaks to us every hour, if we will only tune in."
George Washington Carver

Remember that you are part of nature, too. You are beautiful and blessed and are loved more than you can imagine.

Method #14

Tune in to God with silence

All of the preceding methods have led to this point—the place of silence.

In our busy world with our busy lives and busy thoughts, it requires an effort to carve some time out of your day to experience silence.

Several times it is written that Jesus went out by himself to the wilderness or the mountain or a secluded place—to be alone, to tune in to God.

It is certain that Jesus, being an expert on the scriptures and teachings of His culture, knew and taught the value of silence.

"To every thing there is a season, and a time to every purpose under the heaven: A time to rend, and a time to sew; a time to keep silence, and a time to speak;"

Ecclesiastes 3:1, 7

"For thus saith the Lord God the Holy One of Israel: If you return and be quiet, you shall be saved: in silence and in hope shall your strength be."

Isaiah 30:15 (Douay-Rheims Bible)

"But the LORD is in his holy temple: let all the earth keep silence before him."

Habakkuk 2:20

"My soul waits in silence for God only; From Him is my salvation. My soul, wait in silence for God only, For my hope is from Him."
Psalm 62: 1, 5 (New American Standard Bible)

"The LORD is good to those who wait for Him, To the person who seeks Him. It is good that he waits silently For the salvation of the LORD."
Lamentations 3:25-26 (New American Standard Bible)

"Be silent before the Lord GOD! For the day of the LORD is near, For the LORD has prepared a sacrifice, He has consecrated His guests."
Zephaniah 1:7 (New American Standard Bible)

"Be still, and know that I am God: I will be exalted among the heathen, I will be exalted in the earth."
Psalm 46:10

Jesus advised:

"But thou, when thou prayest, enter into thy closet, and when thou hast shut thy door, pray to thy Father which is in secret; and thy Father which seeth in secret shall reward thee openly."
Matthew 6:6

Now that we have opened and cleansed our hearts and our minds, now that we have forgiven and been forgiven, now that we have surrendered our will to the Creator's Will, now that we have gotten into the flow of Divine Love, we are now ready to enjoy the silence.

Breathe in and allow your heart, your eyes, and the corners of your mouth to be drawn upward toward the Infinite Eternal Father God. Sigh, smile, and feel your heart beating out Love, Love, Love... And exhale more completely.

Breathe in deeply... and sigh again... and listen to the sound of the sigh... Now breathe normally and notice if you can still hear the sound of your breathing... Just relax... and be still... and listen... to the sound of the silence behind the sound of your breathing... Just relax... and enjoy... the silence..... Smile.

But, if you are like most of us the silence will not last for long. Thoughts will appear and distract you from the silence. Just observe the thought passing by – like a cloud drifting by. And let your awareness return to the vast sky of silence that is behind and encompasses all of these thoughts/clouds.

Just breathe deeply and sigh and let go of the thought and enjoy the silence. The better you get at keeping your awareness on looking up, breathing more deeply, and feeling your heart the better you are able to smile and enjoy the silence and not be as distracted by thoughts, memories, and daydreams.

Spending a few minutes per day in the silence will have profound effects upon your life. And <u>Tuning In To God: An audio guide to the miracle methods of Jesus</u> is a great way to take you to the doorway to silence.

Spend some time in the silence and listen. Listen.

Listen for the still, small voice.
Listen for the Word.
Listen for the music of the spheres.
Listen for the primordial sound.
Listen for the Name, the vibration, of God.
Listen for a high-pitched tone.

Many other people from many cultures and traditions have spoken of the wonder, the power, and the beauty of silence. In the silence you are tuned in to God. When you tune in to God and have less static from mundane concerns, miracles may happen.

"Silence is God's first language; everything else is a poor translation. In order to hear that language, we must learn to be still and to rest in God."

Thomas Keating

"The friend of silence comes close to God. In secret he converses with him and receives his light."

John Climacus

"Silence will illuminate you in God… and deliver you from phantoms of ignorance. Silence will unite you to God… In the beginning we have to force ourselves to be silent. But then from our very silence is born something that draws us into deeper silence."

Isaac of Nineveh, seventh century Syrian monk

"We need silence to be alone with God, to speak to him, to listen to him, to ponder his words deep in our hearts. We need to be alone with God in silence to be renewed and transformed. Silence gives us a new outlook on life. In it we are filled with the energy of God himself that makes us do all things with joy."

Mother Teresa of Calcutta

"It is in deep solitude and silence that I find the gentleness with which I can truly love my brother and sister."

Thomas Merton

"Learn to get in touch with the silence within yourself and know that everything in this life has a purpose. There are no mistakes, no coincidences. All events are blessings given to us to learn from."

Elizabeth Kübler-Ross

"Let me rest in Your will and be silent. Then the light of Your joy will warm my life. Its fire will burn in my heart and shine for Your glory. This is what I live for. Amen, amen."

Thomas Merton

"Nothing is so like God as silence."

Meister Eckhart

"See how nature—trees, flowers, grass—grows in silence; see the stars, the moon and the sun, how they move in silence...we need silence to be able to touch souls."

Mother Teresa of Calcutta

"In the silence of the heart God speaks. If you face God in prayer and silence, God will speak to you. Then you will know that you are nothing. It is only when you realize your nothingness, your emptiness, that God can fill you with Himself. Souls of prayer are souls of great silence."

Mother Teresa of Calcutta

"Silence is pure and holy. It draws people together because only those who are comfortable with each other can sit without speaking."

Nicholas Sparks, The Notebook

"Let silence take you to the core of life."

Rumi

"Make peace with silence, and remind yourself that it is in this space that you'll come to remember your spirit. When you're able to transcend an aversion to silence, you'll also transcend many other miseries. And it is in this silence that the remembrance of God will be activated."

Wayne W. Dyer

Validation from modern science

There is a wealth of research on Mindfulness-Based Stress Reduction and similar practices that can assist folks in getting in touch with Silence. Research has shown that these practices can:

- increase ability to cope with stress
- reduce chronic pain
- improve self-esteem

- decrease symptoms of depression
- decrease symptoms of anxiety
- improve sleep
- hasten recovery from illness, injury, and surgery

Putting the method into practice

Listen to <u>Tuning In To God: An audio guide to the miracle methods of Jesus</u> or record yourself reading the transcript which is the final chapter of this book. It guides you through the miracle methods of Jesus and leads you to the threshold of silence.

Make it a priority to spend some time in the silence. Listen.

Ponder the attributes of God, sigh, smile, gaze upward, feel your heart, send Love, surrender, and enjoy the silence.

Be still…and listen……and know that you are loved more than you can humanly comprehend.

Method #15

Tune In To God with other people

While Jesus often went off by Himself, the gospels portray Him as being with other people most of the time — sometimes thousands of people. Humans are social beings. We need other people. Meeting together with others can be a method of tuning in to God.

Jesus usually went to meet with others on the Sabbath.

"And he came to Nazareth, where he had been brought up: and, as his custom was, he went into the synagogue on the Sabbath day, and stood up for to read."

Luke 4:16

Meeting with other people can open us up to new ideas and remind us of things that are beneficial to be reminded of.

Whether you go to a church/synagogue/mosque/ashram, a prayer group, a club, a concert, or a card game – being with others can be an uplifting experience.

> "Blest be the tie that binds
> Our hearts in Christian love;
> The fellowship of kindred minds
> Is like to that above."
>
> *From hymn by John Fawcett*

Those of you fortunate enough to be in a committed, loving relationship are blessed indeed. Living in a close relationship with another is one of the best ways to learn about yourself, to grow emotionally and spiritually, and provides many opportunities for sending Love and tuning in to God. Being in Love puts one in tune with God.

"And the LORD God said, It is not good that the man should be alone; I will make him an help meet for him."

Genesis 2:18

"Whoso findeth a wife findeth a good thing, and obtaineth favour of the LORD."

Proverbs 18:22

"Therefore shall a man leave his father and his mother, and shall cleave unto his wife: and they shall be one flesh."

Genesis 2:24

Family, friendships, work relationships and even brief encounters are opportunities for learning, growing, and sending Love.

"Be not forgetful to entertain strangers: for thereby some have entertained angels unawares."

Hebrews 13:2

We can also learn and grow from difficult relationships. Sometimes our chief mentors are our tor-mentors. They provide opportunities for sending Love.

"But I say unto you, Love your enemies, bless them that curse you, do good to them that hate you, and pray for them which despitefully use you, and persecute you; That ye may be the children of your Father which is in heaven: ...."

Matthew 5:44-45

Children are people, too and those of you with the opportunity to be around children are blessed indeed.

Jesus loved children. He enjoyed being around them and used their example to help teach about the Kingdom of God.

"But Jesus called them unto him, and said, Suffer little children to come unto me, and forbid them not: for of such is the kingdom of God. Verily I say unto you, Whosoever shall not receive the kingdom of God as a little child shall in no wise enter therein."
Luke 18:16-17

Gathering together with others with similar intent can produce powerful effects.

"Again I say unto you, That if two of you shall agree on earth as touching any thing that they shall ask, it shall be done for them of my Father which is in heaven. For where two or three are gathered together in my name, there am I in the midst of them."
Matthew 18:19-29

"Never doubt that a small group of thoughtful, committed citizens can change the world. Indeed, it is the only thing that ever has."
Margaret Meade

Tuning in to God is an individual's opportunity and responsibility, but gathering together with others with like intent can help yourself and others. Most communities have a variety of Houses of Worship that can provide wonderful opportunities for gathering with others and tuning in to God.

Consider starting your own discussion group, book club, prayer group, Sending Love Club, or whatever you want to call it. Listen to <u>Tuning In To God: An audio guide to the miracle methods of Jesus</u> together and/or experiment with some other ways to tune in to God. In our group we take turns leading the group with an activity, reading, recording, or demonstration – almost always followed by some silent time and discussion.

You can join together with others by saying or intending:

"In the Name of God/Divine Love, I ask that everyone who has ever read or will read this page be blessed and filled with Divine Love. And I give thanks that this is so."

Validation from modern science

Being more social has been shown to improve physical and mental health. Married people tend to be healthier and live longer than unmarried people.

The research of Dr. Dean Ornish, M.D. has shown that having love and intimacy in one's life is the best predictor of health and longevity for heart disease patients.

Research has shown that attending religious services is associated with living a longer and healthier life.

Putting the method into practice

Socialize. Join or start a spiritual discussion group, book club, prayer group, Sending Love Club, or whatever you want to call it.

Pray with others before meals and at other times.

Attend worship services. Volunteer.

Spend time around children.

Bless others. Be a little more loving to the beings you encounter.

Remember that you are loved more than you can imagine and share some of that Love with others.

Daily Practice of the Miracle Methods of Jesus

The methods described in the preceding chapters are powerful ways to tune in to God. Jesus used and taught these methods and they have blessed and enhanced the lives of those of us who have been putting them into practice.

But tuning in to God is something that needs to be done again and again because of our tendency to forget, to get distracted, to get out of tune.

Below are some ideas and practices that work for some of us, some of the time.

1. Get in the habit of spending a little time every day with the intention to tune in to God. Listening to <u>Tuning In To God: An audio guide to the miracle methods of Jesus</u> is one way to do this. This recording was developed to way to put the miracle methods of Jesus into an easy to practice format that doesn't take much time.

2. Read inspired and inspiring words (like this book) that help you to tune in to God.

3. Listen to music that uplifts you and tunes you in to God.

4. Watch uplifting video on TV (PBS has some great shows), internet, movies.

5. Chant.

6. Sing.

7. Tone.

8. Make your own joyful noise unto God. Woohoo!

9. Breathe more deeply.

10. Sigh.

11. Smile more.

12. Spend time in nature.

13. Send Love to yourself and others.

14. Bless yourself and others.

15. Do some of these while driving or walking.

16. Feel your heart.

17. Do the Thank You Breath.

18. Do the Two Greatest Commandments Breath.

19. Do the I Am Love Breath.

20. Do the God's Will Breath.

21. Make up your own breath prayers.

22. Say grace, thanks, a prayer before meals.

23. Say The Lord's Prayer every time you bathe.

24. Say the Serenity Prayer.

25. Look up, sigh, and say "Ephphatha" (be opened) at work, in the grocery store, wherever. Your intention can be for your ears to be opened, or your eyes, or the gates of Heaven, or whatever you would like opened. Jesus did this and a miracle occurred.

26. Jesus said to go into your closet to pray. Well, how about getting in the habit of saying a prayer or making an effort to tune in to God every time you go into the "water closet" (bathroom).

27. Give thanks and send Love to the Sun.

28. Look at the stars and let your mind expand as you consider the billions of stars in our galaxy, and the billions of galaxies.

29. Appreciate and send Love to your body and consider the miraculous things it does.

30. Keep a gratitude journal.

31. Write a book. Writing this book has been a life-changing experience.

32. Help others.

33. Take a little better care of yourself.

34. Ask for help. Ask God. Ask angels. Ask other people. You know how helping others gives you a good feeling inside. If you do not ask others for help you are being stingy and not giving them a chance to get some of those good feelings.

35. Spend time with children and/or have pictures of children around.

36. When you prepare food let Love be the main ingredient.

37. Bless your water before you drink it.

38. Whatever you do, try to do it with a little more love.

39. Laugh.

40. Have fun.

41. Imagine a bright Love/Light in your heart. As you breathe deeply see it expand to fill your body, the room, the building, the neighborhood, the country, the Earth, the solar system, the galaxy, the universe. *Feel* the universe filled with Love/Light.

42. Say "I surrender my will to the Creator's Will."

43. Say "Father, forgive them for they know not what they do."

44. Say "Father, please forgive me for everything I have done that is not in accordance with Your Will."

45. Say "I allow myself to be forgiven."

46. Say "I forgive myself."

47. Smile larger.

48. Remember a time when you Loved unconditionally.

49. Remember a time when you felt Loved.

50. Remember that God Loves you more than you can possibly understand.

51. Smile at yourself in the mirror and send Love to yourself.

52. Try to tune in to God first thing in the morning(the snooze alarm is a wonderful invention).

53. Try to tune in to God as you fall asleep. Maybe use a breath prayer or an affirmation such as "Every day in every way I am getting more and more tuned in to God."

54. Kiss your hand and send it Love.

55. Kiss or blow a kiss to someone or something.

56. Kiss toward God. "Worship" in the Greek language in which the gospels were written means "kiss toward."

57. Send an anonymous postcard or gift.

58. Do a random act of kindness.

59. Say a prayer for others.

60. Say "Father, please bless _____."

61. Bless everyone, even (especially) those you may think don't deserve it, even yourself.

62. Donate — time, gifts, good thoughts, a smile.

63. Be creative. Think up a new way to tune in to God. Please feel free to share your ideas with us so that we may share them with others on our website or in a future book.

64. Make your password something that reminds to tune in to God.

65. Sign up for the twice-weekly Tune In To God email reminder on our website: TuneintoGod.com

66. Say a prayer or affirmation as you walk—one word for each step.

67. Spend some time in the silence.

68. Say "I forgive everyone who has ever hurt me in any way to the best of my ability and I ask God to help me be more forgiving"

69. Every being that you meet, see, and think of is an opportunity to send Love. You are a radio broadcasting out to others that to which you are tuned in to. Are you playing/singing/vibrating harmoniously or discordantly? Even without conscious intention you are either blessing and uplifting others, keeping the status quo, or broadcasting out discordant vibrations. Tune in to God for a few moments per day and at other times occasionally and you will radiate Good and be a blessing to the world.

Send us your ideas on daily practices that help you to tune in to God and we may post them on our website or publish them in future works.

Send some Love also to: Love(at)TuneintoGod.com

The Final Word

Writing this book has been a life-changing experience.

Spending time with these ideas, Bible verses, quotations, and methods has helped us to tune in to God more and it is intended that sharing them will help others to do the same.

We all need to learn to tune in to God better. Or maybe we need to learn to be more aware that we are already tuned in to God.

Spending time in the silence is Good. In the silence you realize that you are always tuned in to God ... and God is always tuned in to you.......Loving you...... And you can feel that Love... and radiate that Love..... if you can pay less attention to the static (worries, apparent limitations) and pay more attention to Spirit/breath, Love/heart, God and his blessings and miracles.

Modern physics tells us that everything is energy/vibration.

"In the beginning was the Word, and the Word was with God, and the Word was God. The same was in the beginning with God. All things were made by him; and without him was not any thing made that was made. In him was life; and the life was the light of men. And the light shineth in darkness; and the darkness comprehended it not."
John 1:1-5

Ponder the possibility that tuning in to God is tuning in to the Word, the Name, the primordial sound, the music of the spheres, the Kingdom of God, the Kingdom of Heaven, the frequency/vibration of Divine Love, the still, small voice. Spend a few minutes per day (or most days) with the conscious intention to tune in to God using some of the methods that Jesus taught and used.

"These words spake Jesus, and lifted up his eyes to heaven... I have manifested thy name unto the men which thou gavest me out of the world: thine they were, and thou gavest them me; and they have kept thy word... For I have given unto them the words which thou gavest me;

Holy Father, keep through thine own name those whom thou hast given me, that they may be one, as we are...

I have given them thy word; Sanctify them through thy truth: thy word is truth... Neither pray I for these alone, but for them also which shall believe on me through their word; That they all may be one; as thou, Father, art in me, and I in thee, that they also may be one in us:

And the glory which thou gavest me I have given them; that they may be one, even as we are one: I in them, and thou in me, that they may be made perfect in one; and that the world may know that thou hast sent me, and hast loved them, as thou hast loved me...

And I have declared unto them thy name, and will declare it: that the love wherewith thou hast loved me may be in them, and I in them."
Selections from John, chapter 17

Remember God/Infinite Omnipotent Divine Love. Look up, sigh, and feel heartfelt thanks. Send Love and smile and surrender your will to God. Surrender your thoughts to God and be aware of the silence.

Listen. Listen for the Word, the Name, the Primordial Sound, the music of the spheres, the still, small voice, the high-pitched tone. Tune In To God.

"He that hath ears to hear, let him hear."
Luke 8:8

Transcript of Tuning In To God: An audio guide to the miracle methods of Jesus

(This is the transcript of <u>Tuning In To God: An audio guide to the miracle methods of Jesus</u>. Reading the transcript will give you an idea of the experience, but we have found it much better to be able to have eyes closed and to listen to someone guiding you through the process. You can record your own voice or download the recording and/or order the CD from the website TuneintoGod.com or from Amazon.com)

May Glorious Great Spirit/God/Divine Love be here.
This recording will guide you to tune in to God using the methods that Jesus taught and used..........
When Jesus and His followers used these methods miracles followed. To learn more details and the Biblical basis for these methods go to the TuneintoGod.com website and get the book.

So sit in a position that does not restrict your breathing.....and in a place where you can safely have your eyes closed...... and prepare...... to tune in to God.

Close your eyes....and relax.....and smile......... For tuning in to God is a most wonderful experience....... And the more you do it...the easier it gets....and the better able you are to *feel*.....tuned in to God.

We will begin with God......
Let us ponder the qualities and attributes of God, the Father that Jesus taught about and was tuned in to.

Jesus described God as a loving Father........as an All-Knowing........All-Powerful......Everywhere Present....Spirit........
He described God as being available to everyone....... who would turn to Him.....
He described God as forgiving....and giving.....
Jesus described God as Love.........Divine Love......... And Jesus taught... that you are loved...... more than you can ever understand...... no matter what you have done in the past.......

So take a moment and *feel* this feeling of being Loved........by the Infinite.....Eternal.....Creator........

And *know* .... that you are loved...... more than you could ever comprehend.......

Next, we will become more aware of our breathing.....for breath is life......and breath is Spirit........and Jesus said, "God is a Spirit, and those that worship Him must worship Him in Spirit and in Truth.

With your eyes closed.....just become more aware of your breathing........ breathing through your nose if that is comfortable........

Notice how your stomach moves........as you breathe in....... and breathe out.......

Notice how the air feels in your nostrils.....as you breathe in..... and breathe out.........

Notice how the air feels cooler as you breathe in......and warmer as you breathe out.....

Be quiet for a moment and notice if you can hear your breathing...

Now we will deepen our breathing....and our connection to Spirit.....

by using the only breathing technique that the Bible describes Jesus as using........

And that is the sigh.......... A sigh is a deeper breath...with an audible exhale.......a long ......slow .... more complete.....exhale...

So breathe in...letting your abdomen expand...then breathe in even more as your chest and collarbones lift.... then relax and exhale with an audible sigh....and breathe out slowly and more completely....pulling in your stomach slightly........

A couple of more times....

Breathe in, letting your abdomen expand...and your heart-region lift....

Then relax....and sigh....and breathe out slowly...and more completely......

Once more....breathing in deeply......allowing your heart region to lift........and then sigh....and exhale...... slowly....and more completely....

Don't overdo it......especially if you are just learning how to sigh.....

Just breathe naturally.......and remember some of the attributes of God we spoke of earlier.......
Remember.. that God is All-Powerful ......and Everywhere Present...... and very, very Loving.......and know....that when you sigh....it is a sigh of relief.......that God is on the scene...... that Divine Love is in charge........that you are loved by your Heavenly Father ....more than you can ever understand………..

Let us sigh again.......

Breathing in allowing your abdomen to expand and your heart-region to lift.......

And relax and sigh.....and exhale slowly......and more completely.............

And as you sigh a couple of more times..........if you haven't noticed it already.........

Just be aware of your heart region.....and you may be able to feel your heart beating in your chest.........................

Breathe in....letting your abdomen and chest expand......... then relax and sigh......and exhale slowly....and more completely.......

If you don't feel it yet.......with further practice of the sigh........as you train yourself to exhale slowly...and more completely......you <u>will</u> feel your heartbeat...........

This is a heartfelt sigh...and it is an excellent way to tune in to God........

And know....that with each breath.....your heart is being cleansed....and purified........

Jesus said, "Blessed are the pure in heart: for they shall see God".

With each sigh......the walls you have built around your heart....are melting........

Just place your attention on your heart region......... And as you breathe deeply.... and exhale slowly and more completely............

Your heart may feel strangely warmed...... or like it is magnetized.....

Just be aware of your heart-region........and notice how it *feels*........

Now we will add a thought or an intention to the sigh..........

Some call these breath prayers......

We will start with the Thank You Breath......

Jesus was big on giving thanks......... And He gave thanks *before* the miracles occurred.

Breathe in and think to yourself "Infinite Eternal Father God" as you fill your lungs and lift your heart.........

And say to yourself or whisper as you exhale...."Thank You, Thank You, Thank You, Thank You, Thank You, Thank You, Thank You, Thank You, ..." with one "Thank You" for each heartbeat..... until you can't breathe out any more........

Let's do that again...Breathing in....and lifting your heart as you think Almighty All-Knowing Father...or any other attributes of God......

And breathing out, "Thank You, Thank You, Thank You, Thank You, Thank You, Thank You, Thank You, Thank You,........as you feel your heart beating in your chest......

This is literally heartfelt thanks.....and its power is difficult to overestimate.......

Again,....Breathe in saying to yourself, "Divine Love".........

And sigh as you intend.. "Thank You, Thank You, Thank You, Thank You, Thank You, Thank You, Thank You, Thank You, ..." as you feel your heart pulsing out Love.....

Give thanks for nature....for your body......and for breathing.....and for the Infinity of Divinity that is God...... who loves you more than you can fathom.......

Give thanks for blessings that are on their way and not yet visible........

And if you really want to be adventurous..........Give thanks for <u>all</u> things......even your challenges.......

Give thanks that you are tuning in to God by being more thankful..............

The next miracle method of Jesus is ....looking up...... Often when Jesus prayed...it is written that he looked upward........

He also looked up just before the occurrence of several miracles..........

So let's give it a try............

With your eyes closed.........just gaze upward......as you breathe slowly...and deeply.....

That's all there is to it....... Don't strain too hard....... Just gaze upward....... with your eyes closed......

You may feel a tingling in your forehead or at the top of your head....or maybe not.......

Don't overdo it.......With continued practice you will be able to gaze upward for longer periods of time and may have more interesting experiences........

When you combine this method with some of the other methods that Jesus taught and used you will surely be tuned in to God.

The next method you are probably already doing....... but we want to make double sure....

If you are pondering the attributes of God...... and purifying your heart with a sigh........and being thankful......and looking up....and tuning in to God........there ought to be some smiling going on..........

A smile is an outward and visible sign of joy within.........and smiling increases that joy.

Your smile is like a radar dish ....tuning you in to God/Divine Love....and focusing that Love into your heart........ so that your joy may be full........

So smile!.......... As you breathe in...lifting your heart.... your eyes...and the corners of your mouth.......Then sigh and exhale.....slowly...and more completely......

Now let's put some of these miracle methods of Jesus together and really tune in to God....

This is the "I Am Love Breath"......
With eyes closed...Think about how Great...and Loving...and Powerful ...... God is.......
Breathe in...lifting your heart...your smile...and your eyes....toward Heaven as you think "I AM".......

And sigh...and exhale slowly and deeply...as you think and *feel* your heart beating out "Love, Love, Love, Love, Love........" with one "Love" for each heartbeat.

Let's do that again!......

Breathe in ...allowing your heart and smile and eyes to be lifted up as you intend "I AM".......

And sigh as you exhale and feel your heart beating out "Love, Love, Love, Love, ..." in all directions..........

Imagine beautiful, dazzling light shining out of your heart... in all directions.......filling you and your surroundings with beautiful Light....and Love.......

Breathe in "I Am"............Sigh and breathe out "Love, Love, Love, Love, Love.........."

Imagine for a moment that you are the Sun.

Jesus said, "You are the Light of the world" and to "Let your Light shine before men".

So just imagine .... and feel what it is like.... to be the Sun.......

Shining out Light.... and Love...... in all directions......

As you breathe... deeply....and slowly......

This beautiful golden Light..... and Love.....

Shine out of your heart.......

Filling you .... with Love ....and Light....

And filling the room......... with Love ....and Light.......

And the neighborhood..... with Love... and Light.....

And filling the whole world.... with Love... and Light.....

Just take a moment.... and shine......

....

You are the Light of the world......

And you realize........that without even trying..............you are fulfilling the two greatest commandments.........

You are loving God with all of your heart, soul, mind, and strength...........

And you are loving your neighbor as your self.........

As you tune in to God.......and let God's Divine Love flow through you...........

You are blessing those that persecute you and praying for your enemies............

You are blessing the world..........and you are being blessed.........

You are like a radio..........whatever you are tuned in to...is what you broadcast out.......

When you tune in to God...........

You are sending out Good vibrations.....of Divine Love...... and Light...... And Divine Love...and Light......surround you......

Just relax ...... and tune in to God .... and allow this Love and Light to shine through you.... After all, Jesus said "*Let* your light shine before men" not *make* your light shine....

As you breathe slowly.....and deeply.........

Know that you are surrounded by Love and Light...... and that you are loved....more than you can humanly comprehend.........

While you are in this loving state.......this is an opportunity to practice an important method that Jesus repeatedly emphasized........ and that is forgiveness........

Jesus was big on forgiveness....and it is one of the keys to being tuned in to God and His Kingdom............

If you are not ready to forgive.....don't feel guilty.......... just keep making the effort to tune in to God.....and you soon will be........ ready to forgive..........

So.....while you are breathing deeply.....and slowly................ say to yourself or aloud....... "I totally and completely forgive and accept everyone who has ever done me wrong...... to the best of my ability"............

Breathe deeply...and say it again...... "I totally and completely forgive and accept everyone who has ever done me wrong....... to the best of my ability"............

And looking upward .... ask....."God, please help me to be more forgiving".........

Good...... Now, with closed eyes, gaze upward ...and say to God....... "I am heartily sorry for everything I have ever done that was not in accordance with Your Will"...............

And say...... "I know I have made mistakes and I humbly ask for forgiveness ....and I give thanks that You forgive me"..........

Take a deep breath........and breathe out more completely......................

And say.. "I totally love and accept and forgive myself"................................

Sigh and say it again..... "I totally love and accept and forgive myself"................................

Good job!..........That can be difficult for some of us......

It gets easier the more you practice........

Take a deep breath and sigh a sigh of relief that you have forgiven others....and that you are forgiven........

Tuning in to God is like bathing.........It is good to do it on a daily basis........or at least once per week........

Now we are ready to surrender..........

One way that we tend to get out of tune is by thinking that we can figure things out better than God can............

So it is a good idea....every day......maybe several times per day......to say......"I surrender my will to the Creator's Will"...............

Breathe deeply...and slowly.....and as you exhale, say....."I surrender to Divine Love"........

Take a moment and enjoy ...... this total surrender..... to the Infinite Almighty Eternal God... ....

Feel the feeling.....of floating on the ocean...of Divine Love......
You are a wave in this ocean.... Of Divine Love.......
Just relax....and sigh.......and smile........
And enjoy this feeling of being surrounded by....... And filled with......Divine Love.... And Light.....

Now while you are tuned into God......and His Kingdom............

This is also an opportunity to ask for and receive blessings for others ....and yourself........

It is usually better to ask for things spiritual.....and let God work out the specifics.......

If we ask for spiritual qualities such as Love, Wisdom, Joy, Peace, and God's Will...

If we seek first the Kingdom of God........then all of these "*things*" will be added unto us...

So let us do as Jesus did.....and look up.... and sigh...... and ask, "Heavenly Father....
May thy Will be done in my life and in the lives of everyone I know.
May Your Love.....and joy..... and blessings .... fill me .... and my surroundings.........
May all barriers to your Love.....and joy .... and blessings .... be removed,.....be shined away.......

Breathe deeply and enjoy the *feeling* that all your needs are met....that you are forgiven.... that God is in charge ....and that you are dwelling in His Kingdom ....

Feel what it feels like to be the prodigal child...... returning to your loving parent ...... Who welcomes you .... And showers you with blessings...... more than you can imagine........

And be very, very thankful.......... and smile.....

Let us give some heartfelt thanks with another Thank You Breath...........

Breathing in and lifting your heart, smile, eyes, and praise to Heaven.......

And breathing out "Thank you, Thank You, Thank you, Thank You, Thank you, Thank You, Thank you, Thank You, ..." as you feel your heart beating in your chest....

Once more........it is difficult to imagine being too thankful................................

Breathe in..... gazing upward and smiling...... and thinking of God... And breathing out......"Thank you, Thank You, Thank you, Thank You, Thank you, Thank You, Thank you, Thank You, ..."

Now we are ready to enter the Silence..............

Just relax..........and breathe naturally..........................
And with your eyes closed.........gently gaze upward..........
For we are seeking the Kingdom of God............
So as you gently gaze upward........just ponder some of the qualities of God.....

God is Good......
God is Great......
God is All-Powerful....................
God is Infinite....................
God is Divine Love.............................

And as you breathe... deeply and slowly.........
Just listen..
Prick up your ears............and listen...........to the Silence.... between the thoughts..........
Listen to the still, small voice ....to the Word.......... that was in the beginning with God..

You may hear a faint high-pitched tone............or maybe not..........

Let us take a few moments.....as you gaze upward with closed eyes......and dwell in the silence.... and listen...
....
....
....
....
....

And if you find that your attention has wandered...........

Take a deeper breath ......and sigh......and listen to the sound of the sigh.... and become aware of your heart...

Then breathe normally ...and listen to the sound of your breath......

Then listen for the silence.....behind the sound......... Just smile.....and gently gaze upward.... And remember that God is Almighty...and All-Knowing.....and everywhere present.....

And *feel* yourself to be in the Presence...... of the Divine Love...that is God.....and enjoy...the silence..
....
....
....
....
....
....
....
....
....
....

....
....
....
....

Now as you allow your attention to return to your breathing………

Take a deep breath….and sigh…..

As you prepare to get on with your day……..or your night………

And try to remember …….every once in a while………. who you really are………
Remember that you are a child …..of the Infinite Almighty God…..
When you remember …… to turn toward God……..
When you remember … to tune in to God……….
You will know……..
that you are loved……..more than you can ever imagine……….

And when you remember……….. sometime during your day….take half a minute and do a couple of Thank You Breaths…. with heartfelt sighs…..
Or a couple of I Am Love Breaths…. with heartfelt sighs……..
Or make up your own Breath Prayers……..

An important key is *feeling* God's Love in your heart region…… and the sigh, the breathing technique that Jesus used, is an excellent way to feel and cleanse and open your heart……..

If you practice these methods that Jesus taught and used…… you will *feel* an energy in your heart region.

You will *feel* your heart strangely warmed……..or magnetized……..
You will *feel* your heart being cleansed…and purified…….
Jesus said, "Blessed are the pure in heart, for they shall see God."

You will *feel* God's Love flowing through you... blessing you and your world.....
Just be still…. And silent….. and you will *know* that you are tuning in to God...........

If you seek first the Kingdom of God... and His righteousness.......your external life will be transformed and "all these things" will be added unto you.

Smile and have fun with these methods......

Jesus came and taught these methods so that you can tune in to God so that your joy might be full and that you may have life more abundantly.......

When you tune in to God with the miracle methods of Jesus you are plugged in to the ultimate, the only Power Source and your Love-Light shines, or God's Love and Light shine through you. Tune in to God and allow this Light to shine away any shadows of stress and limitation. Remember God, look up, sigh, smile, surrender, send love, enjoy some silence and let the miracles begin. Read the book, "Tune In To God: The Miracle Methods of Jesus" and/or visit the website TuneintoGod.com to learn more ways to tune in to God.

Remember Love. Love is what It's all about.

It is the intention of many that all who listen to this recording be blessed and filled with Divine Love.

Bless your heart.

Thank You Jesus.

Orders

To anonymously send a copy of this book along with a message telling the recipient that they are loved more than they know visit: TuneintoGod.com
Or write: The Sending Love Club PO Box 230 Graham, AL 36263

Send a copy of this book anonymously to a loved one. Helping someone to tune in to God is one of the nicest things you can do for them. Send a copy to someone with whom you have difficulty. If they get better tuned in to God your life will be better.

For copies of this book:
Enclose $14 ($10 + $4 shipping and handling) for each separate address.
For 2-5 books to the same address enclose $10 per book + $5 shipping and handling.
For 6 or more books to the same address enclose $10 per book with free shipping and handling.
For CDs of the <u>Tuning In To God: An audio guide to the miracle methods of Jesus</u> enclose $9 ($7 + $2 shipping and handling) for each separate address.
For 2-5 CDs to the same address enclose $7 per CD and $3 shipping and handling.
For 6 or more CDs to the same address enclose $7 per CD with free shipping and handling.

If you want to donate with a cheerful heart any donations will be used to anonymously send out free copies of this book.

Make checks and money orders payable to The Sending Love Club.
Visit our website TuneintoGod.com or Amazon.com for discounted digital versions of the book and audio guide and to sign up for the free twice-weekly Tune In To God reminder email.

Stay tuned! (in to God)

www.ingramcontent.com/pod-product-compliance
Lightning Source LLC
LaVergne TN
LVHW021352080426
835508LV00020B/2249